Parting Is Such Sweet Sorrow:
Saying Goodbye to an Eating Problem

How to Change Your Relationship with Food

LOUISE PARENTE PHD, LCSW, CEDS

BALBOA.PRESS

A DIVISION OF HAY HOUSE

Balboa Press books may be ordered through booksellers or by contacting:

Balboa Press
A Division of Hay House
1663 Liberty Drive
Bloomington, IN 47403
www.balboapress.com
844-682-1282

Print information available on the last page.

ISBN: 978-1-9822-5416-2 (sc)
ISBN: 978-1-9822-5418-6 (hc)
ISBN: 978-1-9822-5417-9 (e)

Library of Congress Control Number: 2020916987

Balboa Press rev. date: 09/22/2020

DEDICATION

To my special husband John

Whose love, devotion, support, and
encouragement has guided me.

To my wonderful sons John Jr, Donald, Steven
their wives and my 12 grandchildren. May the
completion of this book represent that if you truly
want something, visualize it and make it happen.

To John Jr. for his time and patience
reviewing and editing this book.

And to God for keeping me on his path, I have been
blessed and touched in ways that cannot be expressed.

To All of You,

Thanks

CONTENTS

TO MY READERS

THE COMPLETION OF this book has many important meanings for me which I would like to share. I set out to write this book years ago, with my efforts waxing and waning over time. I could not seem to get it over the finish line. Part of the reason is that my husband was diagnosed with Parkinson's Disease. Although we did not let this diagnosis interrupt our lives, it did begin to put up some challenges. Over the years his conditioned worsened gradually. While I was gathering the facts for this book, I began to see a similarity in my life with him. I was gradually but surely losing this man, my husband of fifty-two years, someone who always "had my back." The man that was the father of our three sons and the grandfather of twelve children, was slowly leaving us.

I share this with you perhaps because it represents a catharsis that I need as well as an example of loss. I had to begin to acknowledge, issues of shame, anger, fear, and anxiety, hear my inner voices in order to believe and accept what was and what will be. The difficulty I have experienced to finish this book on loss has been related to my personal life, something I needed to acknowledge in order to publish it. My relationship has been positive but none the less, heart wrenching; it is an example of how loss can affect us at any time.

I share this with you in the hope that it will be helpful. Life with a dysfunctional relationship with food is something to be reckoned with, it is far from positive. As you move through the steps that follow, it is my sincere wish that this book represents a renewal from that conflict-ridden relationship to a balanced, loving relationship filled with realistic and positive optimism. If food and disordered eating has become the connection to the self, I urge you to embrace that positive changes are possible. Perhaps this connection represents those last pounds you continue to gain and lose, or are never able to lose and maintain? For those who starve or purge, ask yourself if this denial of food represents the denial to take in life and grow, could this be you?

With tears in my heart and soul I feel so blessed to be able to share with you my purpose to write this book.

As the author of this book, I look forward to any comments on this subject. What are your thoughts, and do they relate to you and your eating problem? Do you ever feel that change is an impossible goal? Did any of this book's content resonate with you? Would you want to have access to and read a workbook to help you on your journey? In the pages that follow I am not saying that in order to change your relationship with food you must diet or starve and never enjoy food. Chances are that you rarely enjoy food the way you would like to. My wish is that food and eating become normalized and balanced, not as an "all or nothing" experience which leads you to feel it is impossible to attain.

> "Everything is theoretically impossible, until it is done."
> **-Robert A. Heinlein**
> "Nothing is impossible, the word itself says "I'm possible."
> **-Audrey Hepburn**

Thank you for listening!

INTRODUCTION

The Funeral

"Most Beloved Fat Self:

Thank you for your courage and your love-enough to die and let me live. You suffered so much pain and you tried so hard; it has been such a struggle-as far back as memory-the hunger, the desperate efforts at control, the torment of self-consciousness and self-loathing. Always hoping, always trying, and working so hard to change-and the failing, over and over again. The shame and frustration and disappointment. Thank you dear friend, for caring so much and finally letting me go. I'll never, ever forget you. I will always care passionately for the suffering of others who are fat. I want to help them. I want to send out a message of caring-hope. We are together forever, in memory".

(LaShan, 1979)

Don't we all wish that we could just say goodbye to our fat self like Eda LaShan? She shows us the thoughts, feelings and spiritual awareness needed to put our eating problems to rest, but this is just the start. We must mourn our unhealthy self and initiate a decent burial; a time when thoughts, feelings and spiritual awareness are integrated and put to rest.

As a young girl, I wrestled constantly with my weight. I did not take control of my relationship with food, rather, I let it control me. I knew this was a problem and set out to better understand it and help others to do the same. My journey toward understanding started over forty years ago when lecturing for a popular diet program. I could never understand how some people were successful and others were not. I needed to learn more. As a young mother of three boys I started my higher education journey going to college and earned a PhD from NYU, where I focused my dissertation on eating problems. I have worked for non-profits, hospitals, and private practice. I have treated hundreds of patients and along the way learned that ending eating problems starts with changing your relationship with food.

How many times have you lost weight and gained it back or started to lose weight and sabotaged yourself before reaching your goal? How many times have you started to eat a portion of food that led to binging, dieting, purging, or starving?

A quick internet search will reveal the billions of dollars that people in the US spend on dieting and health. Why do all these millions of people suffer from eating problems without success? To grow out of an eating problem and into a healthier life, you must give up the dependencies, expectations, illusions, and attachments to its negative presence. The subject of food, how and what we eat, as well as our body weight, has been experienced in one way or another since birth. What we eat, how we eat it, alone or with others, during good times and bad times, are realities that can change throughout a lifetime. Your relationship with food begins as a fetus and follows you into old age.

To change your relationship with food you must work through and grieve loss. A change in one's eating presents an emotional loss, sometimes manifested in feelings of emptiness. If this loss is not grieved, mourned, and accepted, the old negative eating patterns and weight often resurface. This book is my attempt to help you to grapple with this all- too- common problem, specifically from the perspective of loss. It is my modest contribution and attempt to further understand and treat the complexities of eating problems.

A constantly resurfacing negative eating pattern is often extremely painful, psychologically, emotionally, physically, and spiritually. This loss of control, whether it is weight gain, binge eating, anorexia, or bulimia, leads to despair and hopelessness. Through an in-depth understanding of loss, together with grief work, one can better equip themselves to journey through this web and achieve positive change.

We will focus a bit more heavily on overeating and binge eating, however the principles apply to bulimia and anorexia as well.

Along the way, I will guide you through six steps to help you change your relationship with food and address your eating problem once and for all. The common thread that links all eating problems is the desire to be "thin enough." Eating problems include disordered eating, dysfunctional behaviors such as overeating, rigid dieting, starving, purging, binge eating, and the use of external controls such as diet pills, diet programs, surgery, etc...

The six step template I introduce is not a "how to" checklist, but rather a tool to help you understand where you are in your journey. It is designed to help you recognize where you are stuck in order to continue to progress to a healthy relationship with food.

Throughout this book I will use case examples. Every name is false and any correlation to an actual person in its entirety is purely coincidental. The only exception is the lead in quote from

Eda LaShan's actual experience with loss and food. That is her story, but it beautifully exemplifies many stories and the main theme of this book.

Life offers an understanding of how you can work toward and achieve a goal, but it isn't until you fully recognize that you have the answer within you that you can experience it.

PART 1

PREPARING TO CHANGE

> "Life belongs to the living, and he who lives
> must be prepared for changes."
> **Johann Wolfgang von Goethe**

EATING PROBLEMS

- Are you ready and willing to understand and change your relationship with food?
- Are you ready to focus on the feelings of loss that will surface?
- Are you willing to grieve that which surfaces as you go forward?

THERE IS A paradox that exists in messages regarding food and weight, on one hand we are constantly encouraged to seek an abundance of food, yet on the other hand we constantly struggle to be thin. We are bombarded with supersize portions of drinks and food reflecting one message, and then we receive the message that we must be thin at all costs. This leads to the all or nothing approach to food which, in turn, leads to the diet mentality. The diet mentality leads to a web of prohibition where you cannot eat anything that is not part of the diet. Over the years, I constantly saw that the more someone restricted and deprived themselves of food, the more they wanted it. Often this leads to excessive binge eating.

We see binge eating in most individuals who are overweight, or obese, as well as those suffering from Bulimia. Anorexics do not typically binge eat, rather they compulsively starve themselves.

The overweight person who falls into the diet mentality often loses weight only to regain some or all of it back. They enter a realm of struggle, excitement, and despair.

Do any of these quotes sound familiar to you?

"I don't eat that much."

"I don't want to give up my eating problem and everything that comes with it."

"I am so ashamed of myself."

"I will eat only 400 calories a day."

"I feel so empty."

"I will start my diet tomorrow."

"I have tried everything; surgery is my only other solution."

"I feel terrible that I must give up something that has been the source of comfort so often."

"Food has been my lifeline."

"I do eat – a few lettuce leaves and peas are sufficient."

I hear quotes like this from many people that try and repeatedly fail to lose weight.

We are in a health crisis with roughly 2.8 million people around the world dying from causes related to obesity every year. The problem is real, but the solution is not easy. People are dieting and losing weight, only to stop and regain it. This is called rebound dieting. For many, the constant struggle with weight loss leads them to seek a surgical solution. They use one of three surgical procedures – gastric bypass, laparoscopic gastric banding, or vertical sleeve gastrectomy. Surgery appears to be a miracle cure; unfortunately, many patients regain their weight eighteen to twenty-four months after surgery. Many patients that I have seen then seek treatment after gaining their weight back. Whether losing weight through bariatric surgery or not, successful results depend on the individual's willingness to adapt to a long-term healthy eating plan including regular physical activity. Having surgery is only the first step; the journey that follows will determine your success to lose weight and maintain it. In order to make this journey successful, we must investigate issues of loss.

Food is fundamental to life. Food and the person who prepares it often get equated with love. It is a deeply complex issue for all of us, which is the reason why it is fraught with emotion. Throughout the years, I worked with individuals who were overweight, or suffered from compulsive eating, binge eating disorder, bulimia, or anorexia. Although they often followed the same programs and had similar circumstances, individual success rates differed dramatically. In my quest to understand this, I studied culture, genetics, dieting and starvation, neurological, emotional, and psychological factors. Despite all my exploration, there appeared to be something missing. Katherine Zerbe (2003) an expert in the field that I admire, notes that fixating on weight represents the denial of experiences lost as well as any regrets we have had. After years of studying eating problems and treating hundreds of patients, I realized that loss and grief is often that missing piece for many. This is necessary to make their change permanent.

In closing this chapter, again I ask you:

- Are you ready and willing to understand and change your relationship with food?
- Are you ready to focus on the feelings of loss that will surface?
- Are you willing to grieve that which surfaces as you go forward?

Points to Remember:

1. There is a paradox that exists between the mixed messages regarding food and weight. A serious conflict exists between the abundance of food and the struggle to be thin.

2. The increase in eating problems is astounding and keeps climbing.

3. Fixating on weight represents the denial of experiences lost as well as any regrets we have had.

4. Often the study of loss and grief is the missing piece needed to change our relationship with food and the disorder.

LOSS ALONG THE LIFE CYCLE AND ITS CONNECTION TO EATING AND RESILIENCE

The Story of Jenny

"THE SKY BURST into flames so high the naked eye couldn't see, the black smoke came bellowing down, and then all was black, empty, and painful." This is how Jenny described what she experienced as the New York Twin Towers fell on 9/11. She saw this from the Staten Island Ferry as she was about to embark on her daily trip to work. This particular day, she was going in later than usual, something she was and continues to be grateful for. However, the unbelievable happened, her daughter Gina was one of those who perished.

When Jenny entered treatment four months later, she still had not returned to work; although stricken with grief, she tried to rely on her faith to understand why her twenty-three year old daughter had perished as a result of this disaster. Her grieving family became extremely concerned because Jenny insisted that she had "come to terms" with this. They witnessed a strong woman who was in denial of her fear, anxiety, and anger. Jenny, who was of Italian descent, always experienced food as love but now she was eating in a way they had never witnessed. Within three months she had gained over thirty pounds and continued to use food, which was her shield from feelings, to hide from what she could not come to terms with. At first, she denied the need to seek treatment, but when an aunt became ill with cancer and begged Jenny to speak to someone, she finally conceded. Jenny entered my office with a big smile and immediately insisted she was "really ok". She told me she was doing this for her aunt and her family. Initially I saw a lovely woman, neatly dressed, nicely made up, and overweight by approximately forty-five pounds. As I looked into her eyes, I saw pain and sadness. I felt overwhelmed by the feelings I experienced, the ones she denied and needed to bury, hopefully until now. During treatment she remained staunch and void of feelings, but she was able to intellectually explain all the events leading up to and after that day. Her plan was to come in two or three times to satisfy her family; I didn't agree or disagree but helped her to talk, that was what we did for approximately five weeks. During that time, she was testing me while testing herself; I believe our sessions were not threatening to her. There was a comfort and connection developing. It appeared easy for her to talk about so many things including the way food helped her to feel safe and connected to Gina.

One day Jenny walked in, reported her aunt was failing and began to sob, something up to this point she had not allowed herself to do. She cried for weeks, I listened and tried to hold back my own tears. The pain in her heart was contagious. This began the grief work she had repressed. After several months she began to realize that her relationship with food was a false replacement for "her Gina". Feelings of anger, anxiety, and fear began to surface. There was a level of shame Jenny experienced because she survived the death of her daughter. She began to explore, understand, and feel the anger, anxiety, fear, and shame she had held internally. One day her visit to the cemetery felt different, she would always have the memories of her daughter, love her, and deeply miss her; she was on the path to emotionally say good-bye. She began to grieve her loss.

During the months that followed, she focused on the multiple stages of loss - her relationships with people as well as with food. She began to see the importance of letting go of the negative and destructive relationship she had with food. She was able to recognize that she had abused food in some form for years. The tragedy she experienced with her daughter caused this relationship to intensify. She began to recognize that the excessive food and weight temporarily shielded her from her pain. Now she was ready and willing to understand and change her relationship with food.

She returned to work and decided to put together a box that included symbols of her abusive relationship with food. This box also included treasures that represented "her Gina". She wanted to toss it into the river from the ferry, the same ferry she was about to embark on that tragic day. She described this experience as "gut wrenching", painful and yet freeing. This represented the beginning of another phase in her life, one that would always include the deep love and memories of her daughter. This box of memories also represented a new relationship with food that would be healthy, mindful, and enjoyable; this continues today. This is a true example of Jenny's resilience and willingness to acknowledge and feel the emotions that she experienced throughout life.

While working with people like Jenny I experienced a full range of feelings and emotions. They allowed me into their life, and I feel so honored and touched by their stories. There is no more significant and important experience one can have, I thank you all.

As you read this story, it is clear how Jenny's specific life and loss affected her eating, and how, working through feelings that surfaced while changing her relationship with food was pivotal for her success.

LIFE CYCLE

LET'S EXAMINE THE ongoing losses one may experience throughout the life cycle. As we transition through the life stages, we experience losses and new beginnings. However, if you experienced significant losses and trauma of any type, you may have turned to food by overeating or restrictive eating. Reaction to loss differs from person to person. I have met people who cannot eat after a loss, or after a change in their life; others use food as a cushion to repress the discomfort or pain of the loss and its impact on their life.

Eric Erickson (1980), a well-known psychologist, wrote about identity and the life cycle. He stressed identity changes and the impact of self-image throughout the life cycle. He developed eight stages which include psychosocial crises, and their relationships to loss.

His eight stages of psychosocial development are Trust vs. Mistrust, Autonomy vs. Shame/Doubt, Initiative vs. Guilt, Industry vs. Inferiority, Identity vs. Role Confusion, Intimacy vs. Isolation, Generativity vs. Stagnation, and Integrity vs. Despair. He stated that over our life span from infancy through late adulthood there is a crisis or task that needs to be resolved. He believed that healthy completion of each task leads to a healthy personality. If this is not completed, feelings of inadequacy are the result.

Take time to focus on the effect that loss has on your body, food consumption and the relationship between them. When you were younger was your ideal body realistic? As you matured did you face aspects of loss as things changed? Have you adapted to and accepted who you are as well as your self-image? Is your ideal body today realistic?

RESILIENCE

DURING THE COURSE of maturational transitions, you experience stress related to change. This happens whether the change is positive, negative, minor, major, easy, or difficult. Often traumatic experiences such as abuse, loss of loved ones, loss of health and dreams lead to eating problems. Jenny demonstrates trauma and resilience. Changing your relationship with food often requires a great deal of self-reflection, movement, grief, resilience, and the ability to understand and find meaning in life events. We need to normalize ambivalence and develop hope to insure positive change. To be resilient is to be able to recover from illness, depression, or any adversity. Eating problems and the steps needed to change are intense and powerful; the change in the eating behavior is most definitely an example of resilience. You may have experienced this in your life. The pain that an eating problem causes permeates many parts of life along with the lives of those who care and worry about you. Perhaps people have said to you, "just eat less and you will lose weight," "we don't understand why you are starving, just start eating a little more," "don't you want to be healthy?" "You have such a beautiful face if only...," "I'll buy you anything you want, just change this behavior."

Eating problems are not limited to the United States; they are seen in other cultures, and countries, across all races, genders, and lifestyles. These factors contribute to the ease or difficulty of making a change. A decision to truly change is powerful and deserves self-acknowledgment and self-love. Help and encouragement from others is golden, in many ways it may represent a guiding light, yet only you can make the change. The process of grieving the old eating patterns, working through the loss and recovery is needed. As you work to change your relationship with food and grieve the loss, you will find the energy and optimism to live a life you want. For many years you may have been absent from life, experiencing a state of isolation from the future or a life with many limitations. As you know common threads that link eating problems are the drive for thinness, low self-esteem, poor body image, mood intolerance and perfection. It is my hope that you will say good-bye to the unrealistic.

As you change your relationship with food, issues of loss will surface. Hopefully, you will be open to this, and use this book as a guide to a newer, healthier you.

"Life brings with it an understanding of how you can work toward and achieve a goal, but it isn't until you fully recognize that you have the answer within you that you can move."

Points to Remember

1. The story of Jenny exemplifies how one's specific life losses effect eating problems.

2. As we transition through the life stages, we experience loss and new beginnings. However, if you experienced significant losses and trauma of any type, you may have turned to food by overeating or restricted eating. Reaction to loss differs from person to person.

3. Changing your relationship with food requires a great deal of self-reflection, movement, grief, resilience, and the ability to understand and find meaning in life events. There is the need to normalize ambivalence and develop hope. These are aspects of positive change.

4. The process of grieving the old eating patterns, working through the loss, and recovering requires resilience. For many years, you may have been absent from life, perhaps experiencing a state of isolation from the life you want.

5. "Life brings with it an understanding of how you can work toward and achieve a goal, but it isn't until you fully recognize that you have the answer within you that you can move".

RELATIONSHIPS

IN LIFE, WE experience many types of relationships. Some can be close connections between two people formed by emotional bonds, shared interests, mutual experiences, and proximity. A few examples are friendships, partnerships, casual relationships, romantic relationships, and family relationships. Exploration into friendships show that they can be close, emotional, open, closed, loving, romantic, oppositional, dependent, and abusive to name a few. Many provide a means to experience deep fulfillment and yet some little to no fulfillment. Relationships are formed from birth and throughout life. The nature of these relationships may be consistent or inconsistent. As we journey through life the connections we have had may no longer be experienced as they once were.

Sometimes life dictates whether you want the relationship to change, remain as it has been or end. There has been a plethora of books written on relationships of all types. Some focus on how to develop and keep a relationship as well as how to change one, especially if it has been abusive. A loss is experienced when a relationship ends, whether unexpected, expected, wanted, or feared. Each one of us experiences loss differently; it is individual and fraught with thoughts and feelings one may never have experienced in the past.

I believe we develop a relationship with food, do you? Are you happy with that relationship? What does it signify? How do you live with it? Is it loving, fulfilling, absent, abusive? Only you can explore and acknowledge that food and the way you eat food is something you want to change. Food may signify love, pain, escape, sharing, loneliness, etc.

- Food is not the culprit, but your relationship with food needs to change
- Please ask yourself if your relationship with food has been abusive, obsessive, or excessive?
- Does your relationship with food include patience, honesty, respect, and kindness?

If you are reading this book you have probably read dozens of books on eating problems, joined, or started multiple diet groups, exercise programs, have been in outpatient and/or inpatient facilities for your eating issue. Perhaps you were successful only to revert to your old habits. I know how terrible that must have felt. In some cases, food represents a safety buffer against making decisions or recognizing your strengths or struggles.

Part of the change in your relationship with food is loss. It entails losing the behavior you have used for what might seem "forever". It is important to recognize that you may experience a feeling of emptiness. This behavior has been a part of you for months, days, years. We sometimes become comfortable with the discomfort. You are reading this book; thus, you are no longer comfortable with it. Be aware of this and use the teachings in this book to help you work through it.

Changing your relationship with food opens one to a new lease on life. It can be exciting; it may represent a form of starting over and can become a healthy habit. Ask yourself what you truly crave. Remember you deserve a relationship with food that includes honesty, patience, respect, kindness, and peace.

Points to Remember

1. In life we experience many types of relationships. When a relationship ends, whether unexpected, expected, wanted, or feared, a loss is experienced. Each one of us experiences loss differently; it is individual and fraught with thoughts and feelings one may never have experienced in the past.

2. We develop a relationship with food, do you? Are you happy with that relationship? What does it signify?

3. Be aware that you may experience a feeling of emptiness, prepare for this and work through it.

4. You deserve a relationship with food that includes honesty, patience, respect, kindness, and peace.

TO CHANGE OR NOT TO CHANGE

SIT BACK AND ask yourself what your relationship with food has been. Focus on times when you worked to change your eating problem. Did you? Were you successful? Did you return to your old habits? How did you feel during these times? Were you able to stay with your feelings? Did you stay focused or did you look for another program, diet, etc.?

You may have looked to an old diet method or looked to the newest trending weight loss methods. By using these programs, you were relying on a form of external control. You need to tune into and strengthen yourself, your internal control. YES, THE ANSWER IS WITHIN YOU! But you need to embrace this, believe it and stay the course. While staying the course you will experience some, or all, of the steps in the outline that follows:

In my treatment with people I suggest that they focus on my **Stop**, **Look**, and **Listen** concept.

- **Stop** when you are about to eat.
- **Look** at what is going on with you; look at what is happening around you.
- **Listen** to yourself, yes yourself. We experience internal messages if you listen for them.

Remember eating, overeating, binge eating, and starvation are usually not primarily about food. Rather these conditions are about how you process your thoughts and feelings. When you change how and what you eat, the issue of change represents a loss. Please stay focused, the need to grieve that loss is the missing link.

It is my hope that this book will help you to reaffirm that you want this relationship to change. Food will still be in your life, but it will be customized to one that is healthy, filling, freeing and consistent.

Points to Remember

1. Eating, overeating, binge eating, starvation, are usually not primarily about food. Rather it is about how you process your thoughts and feelings.
2. Follow the **Stop, Look** and **Listen** approach.

WHAT WILL I EAT AND
HOW WILL I EAT IT?

TO MOVE FORWARD, experience, and embrace the steps that
follow, one must first establish an eating pattern that you know
is a healthy and fulfilling one.

Remember these words:

- **Stop-** when you are about to eat.
- **Look-** at what is going on with you and around you.
- **Listen** to yourself.

Let us use those words when it comes to the foods you need
to eat to lead a healthy life. There are no "good" or "bad" foods,
please eliminate them in your mind, this is important as you
transition.

If you have a health condition such as diabetes, food allergies,
heart problems or any other health condition requiring specific
foods, you have a real medical restriction to your diet. If you
do have such a condition, transitioning from life before it was
identified to your current state, was a loss. Special health diets can
cause resistances. How you handle food limitations will probably
need to change. I am sure that you, like me, do not like to be told

what and how I have to eat. I usually know what works best for me, how about you? Perhaps you will prefer to:

- **Stop** eating in your old-fashioned way.
- **Look** at what is best for you and plan accordingly.
- **Listen** to how you interpret this need.

You may be one of the lucky ones who doesn't need a specific food plan due to a medical issue, but that doesn't mean it will be easy to change your food choices and habits. Does it feel too difficult, or do feelings of resentment and loss surface? Perhaps this is reminiscent of other times when you fell "off the wagon."

Ask yourself what foods make you feel good, are they healthy, is there variety, flexibility etc.? Decide on a food plan you feel comfortable with, one that is realistic, includes variety, and focuses on food, fitness, and realistic goals. Some suggestions are: Intuitive Eating (Tribole, Resch, 2012), Feeding the Hungry Heart: The Experience of Compulsive Eating (Roth, 1993), The Women's Health Body Clock Diet: The 6 week Plan to Reboot Your Metabolism and Lose Weight Naturally (Cipullo, 2015), The MY WW Weight Loss Freestyle System (Weight Watchers International, 2019), Delay Don't Deny (Stevens, 2017), a Plant Based program, etc. These programs, as well as many others that exist, can be used if you wish. However, if you use such programs be aware of the structure, I do not recommend programs that are too rigid. You may wish to use them to educate yourself as to the best type of program for you. It is my belief that focus should be on mindful eating, becoming aware of your true hunger and satiation with the foods you choose. Focus on eating when you are hungry and stopping when you are satisfied. If you truly want something, **stop, look,** and **listen** to your inner voice. If you decide you want it, have it in moderation and move on. Please do not think that you have to deny or starve the following day. Focus on how you feel while changing your relationship to a healthy program, one which you can and want to live with. You have contemplated eating this way. Now is the time to facilitate this change and act on it.

Once you decide on the best eating program for you, ask yourself:

- Are you ready and willing to understand and change your relationship with food?
- Are you ready to focus on the feelings of loss that, I believe, will surface?
- Are you willing to grieve that which surfaces as you go forward?

Points to Remember

1. Stop eating in your old-fashioned way. Look at what is best for you and plan it. Listen to how you interpret this need.
2. Decide on a food plan you feel comfortable with that is realistic. Does it include variety and focuses on food, fitness, and realistic goals?
3. The focus should be on mindful eating, becoming aware of your true hunger, and satiation with the foods you choose.
4. Awareness, preparation, and action – focus on these.

WHAT WILL I GET IN RETURN?

OK YOU HAVE decided to embrace the concept of loss and grief. That may sound and feel uncomfortable, but it's worth it to overcome the discomfort of all the years you have repeated the negative pattern. Do you recall the discomfort you experienced when your plan to eat differently never quite succeeded?

Loss is experienced by changing your relationship with food. Each step of the following template signifies experiences past and present. Memories, actions, and insights will help release you from the internal struggles that have imprisoned you. Stop the big cover up of thoughts, feelings and behaviors which have defined your identity. Hold on to the belief that "when one door closes another one opens." You need to keep that in the forefront of your mind. The result includes removal from the revolving door you have been stuck in. This result finally feels powerful, your hope rises, and a healthy, positive path is in sight. You are removing the psychological and physical dependencies. It is important that you do not lose sight of this while you are working through, and focusing on, loss in its many forms.

During this process you may experience a feeling of emptiness due to the change in the relationship. Stay cognizant and focused on the positive. Why? This awareness will lead to a healthy journey and prevent self-sabotage.

In Guy Finley's book, Freedom from the Ties That Bind (2000) he states that "we do what we know", "we get what we do" and "what we get from life, what we receive in each of our moments, is a direct reflection of our present level of understanding." I believe that understanding and experiencing loss and grief helps to change our relationship with the dysfunctional eating problem. This helps us to develop an insight that leads to actions and feelings culminating in the attainment of a goal you have worked so hard and long to attain. Why not try some of the suggestions in this book? "To Be Free" is wonderful.

Points to Remember

1. Embracing the concept of loss and grief will direct you to experience boundless positive possibilities.
2. You ultimately free yourself to be and truly live life with more acceptance and motivation.

PART 2

STEPS TOWARD CHANGE

"Waking up Realizing a bottom must be chosen
When the light has gone, the path not seen
The spirit dead and the shell tired
With a glimmer of hope, a glimpse of will
Humbly turn for help despite shame and fear
Go inside the soul to the darkest place
Search for the beauty and truth
Conquer the demons. Experiences shape us.
Attitude and gratitude make us.
Believe in one's self.
And say thank you
For the gift of waking up."
----Jennifer O.

NOW THAT WE have discussed the concept of relationships, changes, and loss, it is time to discuss the template (six steps) to help guide you on your journey. The template can become a vehicle for change; embracing it enables you to recognize where you are stuck. This recognition becomes a major break-through in moving forward. The pace of moving through these steps differs enormously from person to person. Use it as a tool to separate from the negative attachment, making it a vehicle to help you feel more in control. It can help you to recognize and focus on the pitfalls and resistances that follow. The awareness of each step leads to the realization that life can exist without the eating problem. This acceptance is necessary to recover from the loss of the negative relationship, and its manifestations. This begins the healing process along with the belief in, and adaptation to, a new reality.

Each step represents an area to be explored, understood, and worked through, according to each individual's life experiences. Although each step is sequenced, treatment does not necessarily follow the steps in the order presented. Movement between the steps is possible and acceptable, and can be used both individually, and in a group setting if applicable to the situation. This template will be helpful on your journey to say goodbye to your eating problem.

There is duality in each step that follows. One premise is for you to recognize the feelings of loss that each step represents as you change the dysfunctional relationship with food. This must be recognized and grieved for the change to become more permanent. The other premise is to understand and clarify how each step has contributed to the underlying need for the eating problem. This addresses the fact that eating problems are never totally about the food. Let's look at fear/anxiety as an example:

1. You may experience fear and/or anxiety as you let go of your eating problem via changing your relationship with food. In addition, you may reflect on fears and anxieties that you experienced through your life, some may have been due to this disorder. These may have been significant in maintaining the behavior. They need to be worked through, understood, and grieved too. Please remember that fear and/or anxiety acts as a defense against the loss of the relationship with food.

2. It is important to recognize how the fear and/or anxiety experienced have contributed to the development or increase in your eating problem. Perhaps you have experienced significant losses that led to fear and/or anxiety. They could have resulted from trauma, abuse, loss, and other life experiences. If they were not acknowledged, understood, and grieved, they might have been the catalyst to your eating problem.

A component of an eating problem is control. By laying out these steps and referring to them as you work through the issues necessary for change, you will feel more in control of the entire process. This will enhance your recognition of the pitfalls and resistances that surface. This will become a vehicle for change; it can help you to understand yourself and where you are in your journey of life. This recognition becomes a major break-through in moving forward. Please remember that the pace of this journey differs from person to person, as you will notice in the examples shared throughout the book.

The following chapters are the steps that address loss. Loss of the old negative relationship with food:

They are:

Step 1: Acknowledgement of the Problem
Step 2: Shame
Step 3: Anger
Step 4: Fear & Anxiety
Step 5: Inner Voices
Step 6: Belief & Acceptance

Before you read further, I urge you to address the following three questions again.

- Are you ready and willing to understand and change your relationship with food?
- Are you ready to focus on the feelings of loss that will surface?
- Are you willing to grieve that which surfaces as you go forward?

Points to Remember:

1. This template for change includes steps which are significant and helpful for many. Each step represents an area to be explored, understood, and worked through, according to each individual's life experiences.
2. A component of an eating problem is control. By laying out these steps and referring to them as you work through the issues necessary for change, you will feel more in control of the entire process.
3. The steps that follow are: acknowledgment of the problem, shame, anger, fear and anxiety, inner voices, belief and acceptance.

PART 3

TEMPLATE FOR CHANGE

Watch your thoughts, they may become your actions.
Watch your actions, they may become your habits.
Watch your habits, they may become your character.
Watch your character, it will become your destiny.
Ben Franklin

STEP 1 – ACKNOWLEDGEMENT
OF THE PROBLEM

The little world of childhood with its familiar surroundings
Is a model of the great world. The more intensively the family
Has stamped its character upon the child, the more it will tend to
Feel and see its earlier miniature world again in the bigger work of
The adult life.
-Carl Jung

THE FIRST STEP in this journey of change and health is to acknowledge what your relationship with food has been. Ask yourself if you want to change it. What is your decision? What action are you willing to take to fulfill this goal?

The dictionary defines "relationship" as a connection, association, or involvement. We all have a connection, association, and some type of involvement with food. This is necessary to survive and develop. However, as with any type of relationship, you have to ask yourself if it is a healthy one, one that will benefit you, and allow for positive growth, not one that is abusive, unhealthy and negative. If you are overweight or a binge-eater, you do not deny yourself food however you abuse it. If you are bulimic you abuse food but then need to purge it. If you are anorexic you deny yourself food. In each case the reality is that you are denying yourself self-care and self-love. The pain you have been carrying is probably unbearable.

This step examines your relationship with food in its various forms. This is a problem you might have dealt with or denied for years due to any number of reasons. It may be a result of not experiencing or allowing yourself something. It may be a result of having lost someone, or something extremely special in your life. It may represent an emptiness that you have attempted to fill with your eating problem. To facilitate change, you must work through that which has kept the eating problem alive, and then to grieve it. However, the first step is to acknowledge that it exists. Let's explore your early childhood as one example.

The relationship one develops with food can be indicative of a poor and unhealthy connection with your caretakers. This can lead to self-blame, the creation of a negative image and the belief you are deficient, ineffective, or worthless. The ability to relate exists from birth and develops throughout life. If relationships heal, then the lack of a relationship may cause you to use an eating problem to medicate the vulnerable self, a self that does not feel connected, understood, listened to, or empowered. This lack of connection contributes to the starving or excessive use of food to medicate and stuff down feelings too painful to deal with. The need to mourn the loss of these relationships is needed. Throughout life, we experience many healthy forms of attachments and separations, however if they are not healthy, they too leave a void which may be filled with an eating problem. Please note that the experience of positive relationships throughout life can be a conduit to help release you from the chains that bind. In order to move forward, the impact of relationships needs to be acknowledged and understood.

The Story of Gilda

Gilda, a 59-year-old female, started treatment to understand why she never felt fulfilled. She knew that her relationship with food was dysfunctional and caused her so much pain; she was beginning to feel powerless over it. She had people in her life that loved her and appeared to understand her, yet she did not understand herself. Her recent termination of a healthy relationship was another precipitant of treatment. Gilda was born to parents who were incapable of loving and communicating. Her mother led a life of high society while her father, an international businessman, was rarely home. She was raised by a nanny she loved dearly; this represented a positive childhood relationship. When she met people who honestly cared and loved her, she would push them away; this kept her in a place of feeling empty. Her eating problem was a substitution that added to these negative feelings; but she could not allow herself to feel too good or healthy. If Gilda began to enjoy food, she quickly purged it via exercise, water pills, diet pills or periodic vomiting. Gilda's inability to feel love had its roots in the pain she experienced from her parents which began at birth; her eating problem was a poor substitution. She needed to grieve the loss of what she never had. She recalled the unconditional love experienced from her Nanny who died when Gilda was 13 years old. Once she started to grieve her past relationship with her parents, her nanny, and food, she began to unlock the feelings associated with them and her eating problem. Today, through trial and error, she is closer to a life that is balanced, fulfilled, and realistic.

During this first step you must be willing to acknowledge the problem, feel it, and wants to change the future outcome. In Gilda's case, she ultimately needed to feel the loss of her past food addictions. This led to a diet rich with nutritious foods, beliefs, and emotions. During step one, I suggest that you explore and review your relationship with your caretakers to determine its possible connection to your relationship with food. During normal development, a goal of mothers is to have their child grow up, become more autonomous and responsible, yet not necessarily lose them. In the ideal situation, a father helps to support the process and reassure the mother. The importance of nurturance from both the father and the mother is paramount. A father's absence may be due to his own inability to nurture or identify himself as a nurturer (Parente, 1998). This too may lead to a daughter's lack of respect and pain.

Unfortunately, there may be times when the loss of a healthy relationship with a caretaker is repeated in life, if so the trauma of loss is also repeated. How? One becomes involved in relationships which represent a repetition of the early negative one. This leaves the individual void of experiencing the much-needed healthy relationship. The following story of Joan represents someone who had a loving relationship with her parents, however loss reared its ugly head in a different way as you will see.

The Story of Joan

Joan found herself losing weight after the tragic death of her parents in a plane crash. She was a single mother of two children; they too had to grieve the loss of their nana and papa. This added to her feelings of sadness and pain. In the past, Joan struggled with weight gain. When her husband wanted a divorce and refused any responsibility for their children, Joan became overwhelmed and felt abandoned. She used her friend, food, to get through the perils of her life at the time. She found herself binging daily. She knew it helped her to "zone out" from her feelings but she did not want to change her behavior. Joan's mother and father had always been supportive and loving during her life. When they were killed in the airplane accident, she had no desire to eat. The emptiness she experienced could not be filled with any food. She began to lose weight without giving much thought to it. Once the scale showed a loss of 15 pounds below the acceptable low normal range, she began to acknowledge how unhealthy she looked and felt. Joan decided to enter treatment. This enabled her to explore and understand how her feelings of loss, anger, anxiety, and fear contributed to her relationship with food. Her ability to be realistic about food, and the part it played in her life has helped her to stay within five pounds of a normal range today. She also decided to continue to emulate her parents by being a caring and loving parent to her children. She realized that her relationship with food, in its various forms, was causing her to distance herself from her children.

The Story of Angela

I was presenting this subject at a local town center to approximately 150 people, mostly women. During the summary and question period of the presentation a lively discussion ensued. One woman in the audience shared the fact that she never connected her twenty-pound weight gain to the loss of her husband. This was a woman who remained within a healthy weight range, ate what she wanted, but never obsessed about food throughout her life. During her marriage and pregnancies, she remained within a five-pound range. Her weight gain appeared to be an example of repressed grief, something she would need to address. This was a woman who I would label as a "true thin," someone who did not allow food or body dissatisfaction to take control of her life. The loss of her husband represented emptiness, fear, and anxiety; thus, she began to fill the void with food. You might identify with how Angela used food to cope with her loss.

This case opened additional thoughts about loss and its connection to eating problems. I believe that if your relationship with food has been tenuous over the course of your life there is a greater possibility that it might play a major role during life periods that represent loss. This is exemplified in overeating or under eating in some people.

During this step you need to acknowledge the problems which have contributed to your eating problem struggle. They may be a result of many things. In acknowledging and understanding the problems, you will experience many feelings. Why? As you understand the contributing factors of your eating problem you will revisit them. The feelings of loss will surface, this awareness is important in order for you to set up a plan. This becomes a conduit for change.

How? Allow the feelings to surface. Acknowledge what you are experiencing. Remind yourself of the negativity the eating problem has caused. This is when healthy substitutions will be needed such as your healthy food plan, use of music, communication with friends, prayer etc. It is a time to remind yourself what is positive in this change. Focus on what it will mean to be free of the eating problem which has drained you of optimism.

The above three cases are different in many ways, but all represent the part food played in filling the void experienced through loss. They are also examples of resilience in the face of tragedy.

Let us look at loss in its various forms. Below is list of some but not all aspects of loss that may be experienced during your Life Cycle.

1. At the very earliest period of life a loss is represented when there is the transition from the womb to life as we know it. It is repeated when an infant transitions from their mother's breast milk to a bottle, then from the bottle to a cup.
2. Loss of childhood, adolescence, young adulthood, later adulthood.
3. Loss of pets.

4. Loss of people in your life, not only through death but due to life circumstances and desires.

5. Loss through separations such as divorce and death.

6. Loss of a child, sibling, parent, friend.

7. Loss of health, body parts through illness or accidents.

8. Loss of the illusion of a thinner you that was unrealistic.

9. Loss of innocence (this is especially relevant for those that were victimized by sexual, verbal, or physical abuse).

10. Loss of your children as they leave the home and you become an "empty nester".

11. Loss of how you adjusted in a heterosexual world if you are gay, bisexual, lesbian or transgendered.

12. Loss of your identity as an overweight or underweight person.

13. Loss of dysfunctional behaviors when they are no longer needed.

The above examples are a limited number of losses that may affect your relationship with food. Please stop and take the time to reflect on aspects of loss you have experienced in life, and how you dealt with them or are dealing with them now.

Earlier I reference Eric Erickson's (1980) work which stressed identity changes and the impact of self-image throughout the life cycle. Similarly, loss has a significant effect on your body, food consumption and the relationship between them.

As younger individuals you may have had a body ideal that may or may not have been realistic. As you age you face further aspects of loss, how you adjust to these changes can have a major impact on the quality of your life. Are you realistic about your body ideal? Have you adapted to and accepted who you are, what is your self-image? Please note that each step of this template represents beginnings and endings, something we do not give enough attention to.

Saying good-bye to your eating relationship leads to a sense of self-empowerment and resilience in the face of this loss. Once you achieve the steps in this process you will understand its importance for self-growth. Some common threads that link eating problems are the drive for thinness, low self-esteem, poor body image, mood intolerance and perfection. This is a guide to a newer, healthier you.

Step 1 is the acknowledgement of the problem to make change. You must change by saying goodbye to the old to make room for the new.

"A new beginning is possible, like new life in a charred forest."
(The Empty Chair, 2001)

Points to Remember:

1. The first step on the journey is to acknowledge what your relationship with food has been. Ask yourself if you want to change it. What is your decision? What action are you willing to take to fulfill this goal?

2. The relationship one develops with food can be indicative of a poor and unhealthy connection with your caretakers. This can lead to self-blame the creation of a negative image, and the belief you are deficient, ineffective, or worthless.

3. During this step you need to acknowledge the problems which have contributed to your eating problem struggle. They may be a result of many things.

4. Eric Erickson (1980) wrote about identity and the life cycle. His work stressed identity changes and the impact of self-mage throughout the life cycle.

5. Step 1 is the acknowledgement of the problem to make change. You must change by saying goodbye to the old to make room for the new.

STEP 2 – SHAME

*"Once we realize that imperfect understanding
Is the human condition there is no shame in being
wrong, only in failing to correct our mistakes".*
George Soros

A MAJOR GOAL of this step is to recognize the part shame plays in your life. Does it hinder the move from an unhealthy relationship with food to a healthy one?

As you change your relationship with food you may experience feelings of shame. Shame of what you did or did not do that effected the perpetuation of the eating problem. I will explore the definition of shame within the context of an eating problem and review case examples showing how shame deters you from reaching your goal. Focus continues to be on the importance of understanding and grieving the part shame has played in sabotaging movement to a healthy relationship with food. Shame is defined as "the painful feeling arising from the consciousness of something dishonorable, improper and ridiculous, etc., done by oneself or another" (Dictionary.com Unabridged 2019).

While journeying through the stages of loss you may come across and recognize shame. Perhaps you have experienced times with food that elicited these feelings. Whether you are a closet eater or not, you probably feel shameful about the food you eat or the weight you are. You may feel ashamed of your size or the way you see how clothing looks on you. If you have been using some form of purging or restricting, these feelings most likely continue to plague you as well. Shame imprisons you, affects your mind, body, and behavior; it leads to and perpetuates self-criticism. Shame has no limits to age, sex, or culture; it is a major risk for children and adolescents. There is little doubt that body shame is a factor in the development of disordered eating. Cognitively, shame appears as ongoing self-criticism, it contributes to never feeling good enough, smart enough, or thin enough. Behaviorally, it has roots in secrecy, avoidance, self-destruction and withdrawal. It depletes your spirit while injuring your soul.

Shame is a powerful force that can interfere with your development. You may have become vulnerable to criticism and messages related to weight. It may have its roots in infancy. If a baby is not attended to adequately s/he may feel unloved and feel that what s/he needs is excessive and bad. It can be experienced at any age especially if a parents' message is negative and critical. During your childhood you might have been made to feel shame over having ordinary impulses. This could lead to a depressed state. These messages regarding impulses can be manifested in the freedom to eat what you want within reason. As an adult, you might have questions about your right to allow yourself what to eat. Eating is not a crime, but deprivation is. Please ask yourself if you were made to feel shame over your impulses? If so the issue of entitlement can be affected as well. Shame as well as anger, fear, anxiety, and powerlessness can become internalized in the body in the form of an eating problem. This in turn becomes a way to bury the pain. It becomes a false protection. Remember that an eating problem is rarely just about the food rather it becomes a false sense of control and the numbing agent for pain.

Ask yourself, "am I really hungry?" Is the excessive consumption of food, the purging of food or denial of food the false substitution of what the body, mind and heart really want? I believe that the following cases exemplify many of the above points.

The Story of Lorraine

Lorraine came into treatment because she was overweight by 20 pounds. She suffered from binge-eating, was a closet and sugar addicted eater. She felt ashamed of her weight and her difficulty to lose weight. At 19 years old she worked in NYC as a clerical assistant and met the man who she was about to share her life with as man and wife. She lived home with her parents in a household where food was love. She described herself as a closet eater. She recalled nights that she would sneak downstairs to "pig out" on cookies and cakes. One night after returning from a date with her fiancé they kissed, said goodnight, and made plans to talk on the telephone later that night. She hurriedly entered the kitchen and began stuffing herself with the fresh home-made chocolate-chip cookies her mother prepared earlier. At first, she was not aware that her fiancé came back into the house to tell her something. As he entered the kitchen, he saw her eating cookies in a way he had never seen before. She instantly felt ashamed, embarrassed, and wished she could have vanished instantly. Her mouth was so stuffed with cookies that she could not speak.

Perhaps you can imagine how she felt; perhaps you have experienced something similar. This is only one example of how embarrassed she was. She often spoke of how "honest" she was except when it came to her eating habits. Have you felt like a thief, cheat, or liar when it came to food; food that you denied you ate or in the case of the anorexic, food that you said you ate and did not? On some levels, she felt like a stranger in her own home. I believed she was a stranger in her own body as well. She would not have eaten these if anyone else was in the kitchen; she was the thief who did not feel entitled to eat in her own home or in front of anyone else.

Lorraine reported this incident during her next psychotherapy session. The emotional experience of pain and regret helped her to acknowledge that she felt inferior and never good enough during most of her life. She recalled how her father would ridicule her mother's weight, this led her to psychologically join with her mother. She did not want to be criticized, thus her constant obsession with dieting kept her in what she believed was a safe space. To lose weight represented a betrayal of her mother; this caused her to become a closet binger. These facts kept her in constant conflict. Lorraine was literally starving herself emotionally. When she returned home the night of her embarrassing experience she was physically starving because she had eaten very little; this added to her binge on cookies baked by her mother. She had not realized what this represented. Issues of separation, individuation, intimacy, and self-awareness could finally be addressed. This became the basis for positive change. She was on her way to say goodbye to the negative and hello to her authentic and positive sense of self.

Another case example of how shame can manifest itself is as follows:

The Story of Jane

Jane, a 45-year-old mother of three, had not been to a doctor since her 5-year-old daughter was born. After questioning her about this, she replied "I am so ashamed of my weight, I never lost weight after my daughter was born. I cannot go to the doctor until I lose the weight." Shame was the overt theme Jane expressed, however, there were many covert themes that needed to be explored and changed during her treatment.

Jane had gained 15 pounds, however, her negative body-image caused her to feel she looked as though she gained 40 pounds. She admitted having thoughts of purging to lose this weight. Although she loved being a stay at home mother, she missed her life as the working women; this was part of her conflict. She didn't feel as though she fit in. She wanted another child; unfortunately, she had not conceived yet which added to her mood fluctuations. In addition, she recalled how her mother, a slim 50-year-old, expected her daughter to be a permanent stay-at-home mother and criticized her for the weight she gained during her pregnancy. Jane, like so many women, experienced conflict doing what she wanted to do and what she was expected to do. Motherhood was a sacrifice she welcomed but her sense of competency in the role added to her conflict. Internally she felt conflict and experienced self-criticism. In entered food, the compromise solution that unfortunately lead to shame; this was crippling. Exploring her anger and shame allowed her to express feelings she had buried. She recognized that her mother's many harsh comments needed to be dealt with; she needed to make peace with her mother, her body, and her food. In addition, a healthy program of eating a variety of foods helped her to lose the 15 pounds, but more importantly, helped her recognize her feelings of shame when they surfaced.

I have heard people express shame as a cause of their problem hundreds of times throughout my career. Our society emphasizes the importance of weight and its connection to body and self-image. A quick look at supermarket tabloids will yield story after story of how a celebrity let themselves go, wondering what went wrong. Is it any surprise that we begin to internalize this constant criticism, and allow it to manifest in our own shame? The above are examples of people who felt shame about their weight and the actions they took to avoid the feelings they experienced. The real shame is how this imprisoned them, causing a form of emotional pain and paralysis, leading to a defective sense of self. Shame robs one of spirit and dignity and focuses on the "pursuit of thinness" instead of the "pursuit of happiness."

Many people have illusions about life after weight loss. They have a magical belief which is not realistic. In part it includes the illusion that all will be perfect once they reach that "special" number on the scale. At this point, I want to stress the importance of becoming aware of your expectations in life as well as understanding how realistic they are; ask yourself if they are your expectations and not that of others. This acknowledgement will serve to limit shame as it refers to weight and food consumption.

There are many theoretical explanations of shame as it exists today, but most agree that it is a powerful force. If you have experienced disordered eating, it may have led to the "all or nothing" pattern of eating. This refers to a rigid behavior of eating. If one does not follow "the diet" exactly, there is a tendency to eat excessively with the intent to starve the following day. This rarely works and leads to yo-yo dieting, increased shame, and a reduction in self-esteem. I believe this behavior is a prerequisite to more severe eating problems.

The Story of Arlene

Arlene started her diet every Monday. If she deviated, she would binge and promise herself to starve the next day. This pattern was repetitive. One day she began to apply the **stop, look,** and **listen** mindfulness approach; we revisited this often in her treatment. As she worked to change her relationship with food there were still times she would revert back to her dysfunctional eating, but Arlene no longer punished herself or allowed her "shameful eating" to stop her from getting back on track immediately. Eventually, she began to forgive herself and utilize the mindfulness approach regularly. She continued to challenge herself, which helped change the dysfunctional cycle. She needed to see how shame had contributed to her past eating issues. She began to express them, feel them, and use them to change her relationship with food.

The use of a **Stop, Look** and **Listen** approach encompasses mindfulness. The Stop suggests that before you react, you back away, exercise some patience and Look at what is happening, what is happening around you, what is happening within you. Look to see if there is something that is obvious or not. Listen to yourself and listen to what is being said. Listen for overt and covert messages. Then determine what would be the Best and most Positive course of action to take. For years I have heard clients state "I am going to do it this time." Shame may be the result if you are overwhelmed and cannot sustain the change wished for. If you are one of the people who fit into the categories outlined in this book, you know what I mean. Whether you want to lose weight, stop your binge eating, purging, or starving, chances are that you will be vulnerable to shame if you do not make changes.

How often have you said "when I lose weight or get to my ideal weight, I will travel…, learn a language…., find a partner…, be happy…" (fill in the blanks)? Please remember that life is in the doing not the waiting until. . . . I have observed that those who pursue interests find that their eating problem mindset improves for the better. This helps to fill the physical and mental void.

Very few people have a life without some regret. We experience a multitude of thoughts and feelings throughout life. It is not a crime to overeat or to eat less. It is a problem when this relationship with the food leads to a decline in a healthy body and mind. We are surrounded by mixed messages and iconic images. This is important to understand and recognize, if not, the shame and pain may perpetuate a cycle of self-destruction.

As you can see shame plays a very important part in understanding and changing your relationship with food. As indicated above shame can perpetuate the need to stay connected to dysfunctional eating. This step can help you to acknowledge how important it is to stay focused to realistically change this relationship to a healthy one. The acknowledgment of shame can release you and enable you to make positive changes.

To recap, experiences that were shameful will resurface as you work toward saying goodbye to your eating problem. It will be very important to be aware of this as it is a main step in this process of loss and grief.

In addition, you need to acknowledge that past experiences of shame may have led to, or intensified, your eating problem. Again, it is a feeling or an experience that you may have dealt with through the use of dysfunctional eating.

Shame is a powerful force, but acknowledging it can lead to self-honesty, openness and the release of negativity. Please make no mistake, this step and the others in this book require courage. Be proud of yourself as you take the next step in this process and ask yourself:

- Are you ready and willing to understand and change your relationship with food?
- Are you ready to focus on the feelings of loss that will surface?
- Are you willing to grieve that which surfaces as you go forward?

Points to Remember

1. As you change your relationship with food you may experience feels of shame. Shame of what you did, or didn't do, that effected the perpetuation of the eating problem.
2. Cognitively shame appears as ongoing self-criticism, it contributes to never feeling good enough, smart enough, or thin enough. Behaviorally it has roots in secrecy, avoidance, self-destruction, and withdrawal. It depletes your spirit while injuring your soul.
3. Shame robs one of spirit and dignity and focuses on the "pursuit of thinness" instead of the "pursuit of happiness".
4. Many people have illusions about life after weight loss. They have a magical belief which is not realistic. The illusion is that all will be perfect once one reaches that "special" number on the scale.
5. Use a **stop, look and listen** approach which encompass mindfulness.

STEP 3 – ANGER

Let us not look back in anger, nor forward in
Fear, but around in awareness.
----James Thurber

OFTEN THERE ARE issues of anger in overweight and underweight individuals. That anger may be masked with an outer shell of smiles or messages that "all is good", but it is resident and very real. The person with an eating problem often reacts to this anger through self-destructive eating habits. They are, in essence, killing themselves with an overabundance of food or without an adequate amount of food. In many situations, patients are angry because they want to be liked or heard by others, and they react by hurting themselves. This self-destructive behavior is not always internally focused. The eating problem can be an aggressive attempt to hurt others, giving the message: "Look at me, see how I am physically growing" or "look at me, I am shrinking to nothing".

When we repress this anger, a toxic state develops. This poisonous toxicity often effects more than our weight. It can include anxiety, psychosomatic illness, abused feelings, depression, hypochondria, and low self-esteem.

The Story of Sidney

Sidney called several times before setting up an appointment. He was a 50-year-old married father of a teenage son and daughter. He was of South American decent and took pride in his family and his ability to provide for them. He started a small business of which he was extremely proud. There was no doubt that he was a hard worker. He tried to be the ideal husband, father, and son. His family of origin remained in South America which was a point of contention. He had weekly contact with them via telephone and the internet.

Sidney reported that he loved to eat, was actively bulimic as well as a compulsive overeater and obese. He admitted that life was extremely busy but not "fulfilling." He always tried to do the "right thing" with and for his family and friends. His battle with weight loss started as a child. He tried many diets but when he was unsuccessful, he reverted to the binge-purge cycle in the hopes of losing and not gaining more weight. This was his secret from all who knew him as well as his family. He was mildly depressed however his repressed anger was visible in treatment. Sidney did not think that anyone heard anything he said, it was as though it was him against the world. His sadness and conscientiousness were extremely compelling. It became evident to him that although he tried to do the "right thing" he questioned if anyone appreciated or truly listened to him.

During Sidney's treatment he recognized that the thought of giving up his disordered eating presented many questions, concerns, and feelings of anger. As he continued to recognize this and make positive changes, his anger subsided and the thought of changing his relationship with food began, the first of which was letting go of his binge/purge behaviors. Once he began to allow himself to expect more for himself and from others, he rarely needed to use his disordered eating. However, there were times that he would come into a session and complain how unfair something was, he was frustrated because he no longer had his secret tool to numb himself. He knew that food, as he used it, replaced the feelings of anger that he still grappled with. He began to experience control over life situations that he was never able to in the past. His courage to work on this diminished his need to sustain his negative relationship with food and the anger that accompanied it. Sidney's new sense of self and healthy entitlement led those who knew him gain respect for him. His ability to respect himself could no longer be diminished by anyone or anything.

The emotion of anger will surely surface when saying goodbye to your eating problem. It will be important to be aware of your feelings and believe that you can enjoy life without abusing, purging, or restricting food.

Some forms of anger that may surface are:

1. There often is connection to food and the person who prepared it, most likely a parent or caretaker. This anger toward that individual may be replaced by food and your dysfunctional eating. Your abuse of food may be representative of the "I have had enough" attitude.

    Look at the intergenerational focus on food. For some people food was and is considered a main focus of life. There are those who sabotage or use food as love. In either case, food can become a force of domination and tyranny.

2. Perhaps there is anger that you must change your relationship with the food. This change represents a loss. Remember food has been your coping mechanism, friend, and foe for years. Do not deprive yourself rather eat mindfully. Do not return to the diet mentality, eat in moderation, become fully aware of what you want. Remember this change is not temporary, it is expected

to be a gradual and permanent change. Learn to trust and empower yourself.

Stop, Look, and **Listen** to yourself. Make the best decision in the situation.

3. Anger during the process of change may surface, remember to recover means you have adapted to the loss and separation of food that was dysfunctional.

4. Anger that some people do not have similar habits or urges regarding food.

5. Anger toward a few (very few) people who appear to be able to eat whatever and whenever they want and remain healthy and slim, not too thin, or too overweight.

6. Anger with yourself that you gave food so much power. You were the child who responded to the power of food and what it represented. You were the good child or the defiant one who used food.

7. Crying about a comment, interaction, confrontation, etc.? Be aware of this, do not repress it, accept it and understand it. Control your thoughts and feelings through this knowledge.

8. Anger with yourself for allowing things to get out of hand.

9. Anger with the negative part of you that used up valuable time about weight.

10. Anger with yourself for allowing the relationship with food to be lonely and isolated, shameful, and depressed,

unrealistic, confusing, and foggy. This food consumption did not make you feel empowered, it was laden with poor self-esteem.

11. Have you been taught to "swallow your pride"? This represents the taking in of anger causing the overeater or binge eater to continue to stuff food; the bulimic to purge that which was swallowed or the anorexic to refuse food because they were "too full."

12. Anger that you cannot use your eating problem to avoid....

Feeling angry is neither right nor wrong because we have the right to our feelings. It does deserve attention and respect (Lerner, 1997). We cannot blame other people, events, or food, rather we must evaluate our relationship, in this case, with food.

Some, or all, of the above forms of anger may apply to you. You may add to this list whatever you wish, it is your list. Remember the goal is to address, acknowledge and change this, not stuff it down, deny, or resist it.

This step is one you will experience, it will surely surface as you grieve your changing relationship with food. It is important to embrace your anger, be honest about it and not deny it. Although it will feel painful at times, it will allow freedom. In fact, you may feel angry that you started this process of changing your negative relationship with food.

At this point you may want to think about how uncomfortable you have been with your eating behavior. Yes, you are feeling the struggle, the push and pull of change. What is more uncomfortable, working on this change or giving into the original eating behavior and the outcome that follows?

As we journey through life, we experience many uncomfortable situations. Perhaps you felt angry with some of them. Did you use food to deal with them? Here again, you might have abused food or denied it to the point of starvation. In order to prevent the perpetuation of a negative relationship with food, caused by life experiences, it will be important to acknowledge that you are working on this and that you can survive it even if you resent it. Food has been the coping mechanism used to cushion your feelings. This is temporary and negative.

Use the **stop, look,** and **listen** approach. Remain calm and do something to get away from the situation. When you do this, you realize that food behavior doesn't help you to deal with the situation at hand. Often writing about these feelings helps one to delay the negative action. These things can help you to get in touch with You, the You that You want to be.

The Story of Hillary

Hillary started treatment in order to stop her binge cycle. She was overweight as a child and continued to be overweight as an adult. Hillary was married to an overweight husband who loved to overeat without any guilt. She was the child of a mother who was always on a diet. She recalled the pain of shopping in the "big girl" departments and starting diets her mother insisted on. She had a brother who she felt was the "special one," he was smart, personable, educated, and thin. On many levels she looked at herself as being the "lost child." Her resistance to change and confrontational behaviors ultimately caused her grief. She was defensive at first but as she began to understand the dynamics within her family and within her life, she started to see how her anger was manifested. It kept her stuck and in pain. Working through her anger over never being good enough, and not having good enough parents, was pivotal for her to understand her feelings of loss. This was step one in her journey. It helped her improve her relationship with family, friends, and food. She knows that she is a work in progress. She has times of struggle but also times of clarity. She experiences anger and questions "why me" but recently she asked herself, "why not me." This represents her way of constructing a bridge to enhanced self-understanding. This helps to change her focus to her strengths, thus enabling her to allow positive people and things into her life. In fact, she has enjoyed times when she can eat without that old feeling of guilt, she has stated "how freeing it feels."

Please try to recognize anger in its many forms as a possible result and stage of loss that you need to be aware of in order to facilitate positive change in your relationship with food.

- Are you ready and willing to understand and change your relationship with food?
- Are you ready to focus on the feelings of loss that will surface?
- Are you willing to grieve that which surfaces as you go forward?

Points to Remember

1. The emotion of anger will surely surface when saying goodbye to your eating problem. It will be important to be aware of your feelings and believe that you can enjoy life without abusing, purging, or restricting food.

2. Feeling angry is neither right nor wrong because we have the right to our feelings. It does deserve attention and respect (Lerner, 1997). We cannot blame other people, events, or food rather we must reevaluate our relationship, in this case, with food.

3. Please embrace anger in its many forms as a possible result and stage of loss that you need to be aware of. This will help to facilitate positive change with your relationship with food.

STEP 4 – FEAR/ANXIETY

"Thinking will not overcome fear but action will."
W. Clement Stone

"Anxiety does not empty tomorrow of its sorrows,
But only empties today of its strength."
Charles Spurgeon

FEAR AND ANXIETY come in many forms to different people at different times in life, such as fear and/or anxiety of success, failure, gaining weight, or losing weight. Changing your relationship with food will most likely involve some level of fear or anxiety.

There is a difference between fear and anxiety. Fear is an emotion induced by a threat; it is a response to physical or emotional danger. Please do not to be afraid of fear, listen to it and react accordingly. Anxiety is defined as a state of apprehension and psychic tension. It is an earnest but tense desire.

As one continues the journey to change their relationship with food, both fear and anxiety will most probably surface. The goal is to be aware of this and address it as it surfaces.

Be aware that you are moving into unchartered territory. When you get closer to your goals, the outcome and experiences that follow may cause concern. During this step it is vital not to let go of your goal. One needs to be mindful and work with the emotions that surface and not stuff down food or deny food.

The Story of Brad

Brad was a 6'4" furniture delivery expert for over 25 years. During our first session he said, "my size has helped me in my job, however, I am about to retire. I know I need to lose weight, but I cannot do this now." His height and size helped him feel powerful and strong. He got pride from his job and the business he developed in it. His concern was that if he lost weight it would diminish his identity and his ability to control many things in his life.

Brad was ready to retire which, in itself, was a loss. He grappled with the thought of losing weight, but it seemed too difficult to pursue at this point in his life. He believed that his weight was acceptable in his profession but might be shameful after retirement; he was confused but wanted and needed direction. His treatment focused on the loss of his job, his identity as a furniture expert, business man, and the loss of his youth. He was looking forward to retirement, but experienced fear of what life would be like. He was also fearful of dying. I encouraged him to focus on developing muscle tone through an exercise program as well as to eat foods he loved but within moderation. I introduced the use of imagery, something he was able to use to his advantage. I asked him to visualize a beautiful book, which I called his Book of Life. He mentally opened it to a page representing his life today. I then suggested that he visualize turning this page over. This represented a new part of his life. Brad had no problem doing this. The next step was for him to visually write down what he wanted to experience in this next phase of his life. The use of this imagery and the steps in this book helped him to cope with change, deal with the issues that surfaced, manage conflict, and say goodbye to his previous weight and embrace the new. He embraced and emotionally accepted where he was and wanted to be.

Brad's story is an example of how he was dealing with anxiety over transition but also the fear of being the overweight retired guy. The introduction of changing his relationship with food added and brought to the surface much of the anxiety and fear he was feeling. He needed to experience and understand this in order to make the changes he truly wanted in his life.

The Story of Lilly

Another example of how transition affects anxiety and an eating problem is depicted in Lilly's story. Lilly, a 17-year-old female suffering from anorexia stated that she wanted to go away to college. The thought of leaving her mother and her life at home was preventing her from fulfilling this wish. She recognized that a major precipitant of her eating problem was the fear, anxiety, and ambivalence of this separation. No one in her family had attended college, this made her feel more concerned, was she smart enough? Did she have the right to do this? Once she realized this, she began to explore the impact this had on her life. Lilly began to make positive and healthy changes. Just as there are various stages of separation throughout life, so is there when changing your relationship with food. You are not ending the relationship; you are transitioning from one relationship and embarking on a new one. It is important to explore what this means to you.

Are you unconsciously afraid of attaining a healthy relationship with food, attaining a healthy weight, and maintaining that weight? Some people experience an underlying terror associated with this change, this must be addressed and understood. Where is it from, when did it begin, do you believe that you can conquer the fears and anxieties associated with it? Please remember that obesity is a slow form of suicide as is anorexia and bulimia.

I often say to my clients that there are times that they tend to "forget" what they are striving for. It seems as if there is a form of dissociation with the process. Dissociation is a defense mechanism used to bury one's feelings and thoughts. You need to become more sensitized to what you want and need, then work through the fears and anxieties that may be associated with this. You have agonized being overweight or feared becoming overweight. There is a superimposed anxiety to change from that overweight or underweight person to a normal sized and healthy one.

The Story of Mildred

Let's look at Mildred's story. Mildred, a 65-year-old female anorexic, used procrastination to delay eating more. Her fear of weight gain coupled with her minimal food intake kept her in this disorder. She continued to defer the action of eating more to another time in the future. Eventually, she realized that this was counterproductive behavior. Her resistance to change was rooted in many things. Mildred came from a family in which her mother was morbidly obese, and her father was slim. She lost 40 pounds as a teenager and remained within a good and healthy weight range for most of her life. As she aged, she experienced many accidents and losses with her family and friends. She began to limit her food intake, partly because this helped her feel that she could control something. These steps helped her to understand the many reasons why her fear of food and weight gain continued to plague her. Although Mildred has a long way to go, this has been a major step in her recovery. She acknowledges this pattern exists, something she denied and avoided for most of her life and is working to change it permanently.

Theodore Rubin (1975) defines fear as the main reason why people have difficulty losing weight and maintaining it.

There is a preoccupation with food and weight, consciously and subconsciously. Regardless of the food you eat, chances are that you are aware of the quantity of the food. Most likely you are preoccupied with your weight on the scale. Dr Rubin wrote that while having a business lunch with a client he noted that his client threw out the remaining part of his burger, he stated "I felt a sense of loss when he threw it out." Although he had already eaten his lunch, the impact of seeing someone throw away food was disturbing to him.

Fear can also exist once you put into action the necessary tools needed to change and maintain the new relationship with food. Joan's story exemplifies this.

The Story of Joan

Joan was a 53-year-old female who spent a good part of her life on and off diets. She believed she could lose and maintain her weight loss by dieting five days a week and eating everything she wanted on the weekend. She did not want to recognize the fact that she needed to exercise limits on the weekend. She insisted that eventually she would get to her goal weight this way. Even when she tried to eat any average portion of food there was always a reason "not to." There were times that her method of eating helped her to maintain her high weight; however, she gradually began to gain additional weight; when this happened, she was depressed and disappointed in herself. We discussed the importance of adapting some structured eating on the weekend, but she wanted to put this method off, she was "not ready to make any changes yet." The success she expected did not nor could not materialize, this was unrealistic. Joan realized she was procrastinating. Why? She was fearful of making such a change. Joan began to realize that the stress she experienced was greater than actually making the changes she wanted. Our treatment helped her to identify her fears and anxieties of letting go of her old habits. Using these steps, she recognized patterns that were dysfunctional. Her fear lessened as she let go of her old habits. She recognized that she had been tired of repeating the pattern of destruction she lived with for so long.

A key factor for change is to understand how the problem has been sustained. Often there are unconscious compulsions which constitute a fear of thinness. As you work on these steps of loss, I believe that the insight to change on a conscious and unconscious level will be a driving force.

In addition, other fears include the real possibility that weight represents the big cover up, whereas thinness represents exposure. Eating compulsively is neurotic and powerful. Neuroses are the aberrated, deviated ways one learns to cope with security and anxiety.

In general, confronting fear is courageous. To confront fear may feel risky and lead to depression. At this time, isn't it important for you to make the change in your relationship with food, what do you have to fear but fear itself? In most cases, the eating problem individual fears change because their identity is wrapped up in these disorders. To change their relationship with food may feel overwhelmingly frightful and lonely. This represents a loss of the identity that you have had.

We all know a person that is always on a diet. When visiting friends and relatives they ask her questions like "can you eat this." One part of her wants to play that down yet the other part is pleased and relieved. The anorexic fears the acknowledgement of her disorder. The bulimic often questions if they want to change this behavior, but eventually, physical and mental exhaustion take their toll. The binge-eater and compulsive overeater get caught up in the "diet mentality," they become victim of "all or nothing" behavior and continue to look for external stimulus, namely the next diet or exercise program to be the answer that it rarely is. The answer is to acknowledge and work from the internal/ self-stimulus.

We need food for survival; the goal is not to deny, rather it is to nourish with food that is healthy and enjoyable. Eating this way nourishes the body, mind, and soul. Before you can do that, you must honestly know what food represents to you and what your relationship with it is. The importance to care for, respect, and love yourself needs to be primary. What does being a healthy weight and not obsessing about food and weight mean to you? As I stated above, you have a relationship with food, there is meaning in it as well as comfort and pain. Do you want it to be a healthy relationship? Does the thought of this represent a disloyalty to it? Many people that I have worked with have shared this belief. Eda LaShan (1979) wrote that she worried if she got thin and stopped eating, too many happy childhood memories would disappear "to deny the pleasure afforded by food would be to deliberately wipe out the memories of childhood-it would be a kind of "disloyalty"...

Here again we see that through the process of changing your relationship with food, fears and anxieties will surface and need to be dealt with.

Please be aware of the fact that eating problems can develop and do develop due to life and life situations brimming with fear, anxiety, and destruction. It is important to embrace the fact that we are not free from the capacity to experience fear and anxiety. The goal is that we become free from the fear that binds us. When we become aware of it, and acknowledge it, we feel a sense of freedom not experienced before. This becomes part of the template for change. Remember being aware of the fear or anxiety is the first step toward changing it. Each step in this template focuses on the use of suitable and healthy coping mechanisms to facilitate the change to a healthy relationship with food and the Self. This clarity leads to a special acknowledgement of what has been and what can be.

- Are you ready and willing to understand and change your relationship with food?
- Are you ready to focus on the feelings of loss that will surface?
- Are you willing to grieve that which surfaces as you go forward?

Points to Remember

1. As with most losses or changes, there is a separation. This separation leads some to feel fearful and anxious. Perhaps the real intense fear or anxiety is that of facing oneself.

2. Once you become more sensitized to what you want and need you will be able to work through the fears, and anxieties associated with it. You have agonized being overweight or feared becoming overweight. This represents a superimposed anxiety.

3. A key factor for change is to understand how the problem has been sustained. Often there are unconscious compulsions which constitute a fear of thinness.

4. Eating problems can develop due to life situations brimming with fear, anxiety and destruction.

STEP 5 – INNER VOICES

"Listen to the inner voice that
allows you to be you."
Elvis Stojko

The Story of Joanne

THE SOUND OF the steps creaked lightly as Joanne descended the stairs. Soon she would reach her destination. Where? In a bag of fresh bagels a neighbor brought over earlier in the day. Smearing them with butter she ate with wild abandon. The ice cream in the freezer aided her ability to swallow them. Then in a wink of an eye she realized what she had done. She questioned how this could be, she just lost 10 pounds on the new semi starvation diet and was determined to continue her weight loss goal. Now fully awake she binged on a cake recently purchased "in case she had guests" by cutting slivers from the bottom of it thinking no one would notice. The voice in her head said, "you blew it so what, eat more and restart tomorrow."

What happened to Joanne? Did she forget what she wanted which in part was the belief she was going to be successful and get to her goal weight "this time." I believe her inner voices battled, but one voice won. Can you imagine how she felt at that moment and the hours that followed? Perhaps you can relate or understand what Joann had experienced.

Throughout my professional career I have witnessed that most of my patients experience at least two voices regarding their eating problem. Some call it two voices, some refer to it as a bird on each shoulder with contradictory messages. Regardless of how it is experienced, it does exist. One voice expresses the desire to get healthy and eat healthy. The other voice repeats negative messages which encourage maintaining the dysfunctional behavior and attempts to reason why this is the best solution.

Is there Hope? Once there is an alliance of these voices, a more positive outcome will follow. In the context of this book the negative voice prevents or tries to prevent one from experiencing a more positive outcome. These thoughts alone can cause overeating, restrictive eating, and all the negative attempts to change the behavior. I want to stress that in this step, Inner Voices will surface as you work on making positive change. You need to listen to these voices and work to develop an alliance between them, so you can change your negative relationship with food. Sounds odd you say, but not really. Once you recognize what is surfacing you can begin to work on ways to experience a more positive inner voice.

A treatment modality that I find useful in understanding the above situation is an integrative approach to individual psychotherapy called Internal Family Systems (IFS). IFS focuses on the relationship between the Self and the parts. Some basic assumptions of IFS are that everyone has a Self as well as discrete sub personalities, each with its own viewpoint and qualities. These parts have a positive intent, thus there is never a reason to fight or eliminate a part. However, within these sub personalities, there may exist pain, shame, fear, or trauma usually from childhood. These experiences may lead to impulsive behaviors such as overeating, drug use, violence etc. The Self is responsible for spiritual development and psychological healing once it connects with the part and heals it, there is a letting go of the destructive roles, this leads to a collaborative interaction. Richard Schwartz (1995) began to explore the internal interactions of the mind the way he viewed family systems. Sometimes these parts become extreme and take on a destructive role. Trauma such as childhood sexual abuse can lead to the creation of internal polarizations which may escalate and be played out in other relationships. Please note that these polarizations can be caused by many things, you should focus on the relationship between the Self and the parts. The goal is to develop a trusting relationship between each part and the Self. The three primary types of relationships between the parts are:

- Protection-this includes protections from harm and pain.
- Polarization-this states that two parts are polarized when battling each other. Each part believes that it must act in order to counter the extreme behavior of the other part.
- Alliance-this is when two parts may be allied and work together to accomplish the same aim.

My experience is that many people exhibit polarization where the parts battle each other to determine how a person feels and behaves. The Alliance that follows indicates that the parts are working together to accomplish the same aim.

An example of Polarization in a person suffering with an eating problem would be when one part wants to eat large amounts of food but is persistent in fighting that part which wants to change what and how they eat. This is exemplified in the struggle with the anorexia, bulimia, binge eating, and compulsive overeating. Each part believes that the other part is destructive and must act accordingly. I want to remind the reader that the parts are all within the self, they are all parts of YOU. My goal here is not to confuse you, I believe that knowing this aids in the treatment and speaks to a sense of self-control once worked out.

As you begin to change your relationship with food you will need to say goodbye to the old nonproductive means used in the past. You will experience a sense of loss. This step will surely surface and represent a major factor in the goal of changing from the old to the new relationship.

The Story of Sondra

Sondra first started treatment as a college student. She had lost over 60 pounds using a local diet club, however the fear that she could not keep the weight off propelled her into a life of anorexia and exercise bulimia. Due to her weight and my concern over her health, she went for regular medical check-ups, sought nutritional guidance, and willingly came in for treatment. She began to experience the two voices in her head, one telling her she was on a healthy path but the other questioning and doubting. Sondra's father lived out of the country making visits with him minimal and limited. She presented with many abandonment issues which led to her eating problems. Treatment was intense and long term but as her inner voices began to work together, she was able to grieve the many losses she experienced. Today, her sense of self is positive; she experiences a healthy, positive relationship. When we speak about loss, grief and her feelings about life, Sondra recalls what she lost during those early years. The acceptance of her relationship with food has afforded her a life full and emotionally fulfilling.

> *"If you do not conquer self, you will be conquered by self"*
> **Napoleon Hill**

Hopefully, you will decide to continue the journey toward a healthy relationship with food and begin to understand that your inner voices need to be heard and acknowledged. In a sense, you are listening to you. In many cases, an eating problem is a way for a person to express that s/he hasn't been listened to. Perhaps understanding this and grieving this will help you to discontinue the use of self-sabotage. That clarity leads to a life in balance.

Please ask yourself what you are truly hungry for. What do you crave, and how do you attempt to satisfy that craving.

Inner voices can cause and add to an eating problem; but they can be voices of reason and positive. They can help or hinder you on this journey. It is my belief that during this process of positive change that you must not forget this. In fact, if you do, there is a good chance that the negative inner voice is gaining strength.

Stop, Look, Listen = Awareness = Positive reinforcement. Let's look at some other examples.

The Story of Justine

Justine, a 50-year-old married mother of a 22-year-old son and a 20 year old daughter, sought treatment for weight loss. Both she and her husband worked hard but "lacked energy" toward each other. Justine was very forthcoming and connected to our work. Her history revealed that she was the parentified child; she was expected to do "all" for her parents. This belief extended to her husband and children. Her life of dieting included trips to diet doctors at the age of 16 for diet pills. During our work together we evaluated her relationship with food, issues of fear, anxiety, anger, shame as well as her determination to change this situation. Her intelligence, compassion and drive were clear. She was an exceptional professional woman and was extremely valued. She welcomed this identity. Her critical inner voice caused her to feel that she never did enough. She has raised two very independent children with good values and ethics. She became aware of how she sabotaged her ability to lose weight, understand it and emotionally feel it. She continues to successfully change her relationship with food. She grieves the loss of each pound as it melts away because her inner voice has become more positive and powerful. The self-critical part of Justine rears its ugly head periodically, but it no longer affects her weight or eating problems as it did in the past. This positive behavior is part of her identity now, not the old one in which she was the girl/women always on a diet but never getting where she wanted and not giving herself permission to feel fulfilled.

The Story of Claire

The story of Claire is an example of the importance of communication with a spouse who was very much part of her problem. One sunny day Claire came in for an assessment regarding treatment for her binge eating disorder. She was far from sunny rather she was pale and unhappy. She was married to Brad, the "love of her life." She never had a problem with weight or food but now gained 20 pounds within a few months. Both she and her husband had relatively good jobs and appeared ready to start a family but somehow, they could no longer agree with anything. After educating her about binge eating disorder, suggesting some tools for her to use, and requesting a full medical evaluation, I requested that she bring Brad into our next session. Brad was clearly worried about Claire and their life together. One day Claire revealed that her mother died on the dance floor at their wedding. This happened while her mother was dancing with her husband. Not only had she not grieved her mothers' death, she blamed her husband for it. Her behavior toward him was like a scolding mother. Although he tolerated this at first, his frustration mounted. The communication between them that was always special was now almost gone. Their trust level declined, causing a lack of desire to be with each other intimately or otherwise. She lost her mother and was losing her husband, in came the binge eating behavior to serve as an extremely negative relationship. Interestingly, neither of them recognized how they were treating each other. Treatment began to take a positive turn at this point. They both needed to grieve Claire's mother. Her ability to say goodbye to her relationship with her binge eating disorder followed. They began to treat each other as loving adults. Claire's inner child changed to that of an adult with an inner voice that was positive and so full of optimism.

Transactional Analysis (Berne, 1961) is a form of treatment that speaks to three parts of us, namely the parent, the adult and the child. Claire had been acting like a Parent by scolding Brad and a Child in her reaction and denial of the death of her mother. The use of binge eating was a screen and used as a mechanism of denial as well. The Adult in us is always growing, developing, and challenging the Self. This is a pre-requisite to an enhanced self-esteem, self-confidence, self-image, and a healthy realistic body-image. It is my belief that acknowledgement and understanding of your inner voices will guide you in this journey of change.

According to Myra Kirshenbaum (2004) when we are born, we are given gifts. The first gift is the gift of Life. You feel, see, move, think, and breathe. In gift number two, she states you were born to certain parents, this life has a setting, you live the life you were given. The third is the gift of You. Ms. Kirshenbaum points out that this includes all of you, not just the good parts but all the parts. All the parts have meaning and need to be accepted.

In conclusion of this Step - Inner Voices, it is my purpose to remind the reader that as you change how and what you eat (your relationship with food), your inner voices will surface. These messages may be negative or positive but there is little doubt that they are part of your thought processes.

I ask you again, now with more emphasis on the positive voice:

- Are you ready and willing to understand and change your relationship with food?
- Are you ready to focus on the feelings of loss that will surface?
- Are you willing to grieve that which surfaces as you go forward?

Points to Remember

1. Inner voices will surface as you work on making positive change. This step suggests that you listen to them and work to develop an alliance between the two. Once you recognize what is surfacing you can begin to work on ways to experience a more positive inner voice.

2. Internal Family Systems focuses on the relationship between the Self and the parts. The goal is to develop a trusting relationship between each part and the Self.

3. Ask yourself what you are truly hungry for? And how do you attempt to satisfy that craving. Some facts addressing those questions are explored in this chapter.

4. Transactional Analysis is a form of treatment that speaks to three parts of us, namely the parent, the adult, and the child.

STEP 6 – BELIEF/ACCEPTANCE

> *"In the end, it's not the years*
> *In your Life that count.*
> *It's the life in your years."*
> **Abraham Lincoln**

THROUGHOUT THIS BOOK I have asked you:

- Are you ready and willing to understand and change your relationship with food?
- Are you ready to focus on the feelings of loss that will surface?
- Are you willing to grieve that which surfaces as you go forward?

Now I ask you: What is Your Belief?

Belief has been defined as confidence, truth, trust, and faith in something. It encompasses one's value system. In order to accept, in this case the ability to change one's relationship with food, I believe one must believe in it as well as believe in oneself.

The Story of Grace

Grace, a 25-year-old female, reentered treatment due to concerns about her eating and thinking. She had lost 80 pounds which was an unrealistic weight to maintain for her. She was gaining some of this weight back but began to panic and was beginning to think that she had to starve or purge to keep it off. Luckily, she put a halt to this by starting treatment again. Grace is a bright, lovely, conscientious, and motivated young adult. The steps outlined in this book helped her to be aware and more in control. This was a wonderful time in her life, and she did not want to sabotage it. She realized that she hadn't forgiven herself for many past actions which included her food issues. To not forgive the self often leads to further sabotage. She knew she was relapsing, something she had to accept and come to terms with.

She believed in herself enough to start treatment again. On some level she knew that the acceptance of what she needed to come to was still in progress. During the course of treatment, she fell into the all or nothing diet mentality several times. Eventually, she found a healthy way of eating. Grace was more able to accept the fact that her weight would fluctuate for many reasons. She knows how her body reacts to certain foods, and she does not panic but rather stays focused. The end result is that her weight and food intake have been normalized most times. She allows herself to live life; this is what fuels her and not her disordered eating. At one point, Grace shared that she finally believed in her ability to change her relationship with food. In doing so, "a negative veil was finally lifted." She was able to see what she needed to do in order to embrace a healthy life, she now rightfully believes she "deserves."

Words cannot explain how grateful I feel to have worked with Grace. I saw her through good times and bad times. She developed a belief in herself which was tested many times. Her strength and capacity to understand and act accordingly was exemplified by her ability to stay focused. Grace and other cases presented in this book are examples of what has fueled me as a therapist and a human being. How fortunate I am to have chosen this profession.

Understand and be aware of what you believe in, that will alter what you believe you deserve. It is important to succeed at something you are uncomfortable with. Perhaps you need to associate with people who are examples of what you want for yourself. Beliefs control our actions thus you need to understand your core limiting belief system; this will help you to feel empowered. Begin to manifest what you want. Be clear about your thoughts and wishes as they will help to alter what you believe. A positive identity can be the outcome.

As you embrace each of the steps laid out in this book it is my belief that you will begin to believe in yourself in a way that is different than experienced in the past. These steps will empower you to continue on your journey of health through consistent eating patterns; you will take more responsibility to achieve this. By now you may be more aware of why this is important to you. This awareness goes deeper than you experienced previously, it can alter what you believe, your decisions, and most of all your actions. When you embrace this program, you will become more aware of what your body is asking for, not just craving. This will lead to an understanding of what your purpose is. Think of the energy used to perpetuate your eating problem. As your relationship with food changes, that energy can be used to enhance your life. These steps will help you to experience and recognize things that were buried from the past.

Please remember that not everyone will go through every step or in the order that I have presented. In order to embrace and accept a life without the eating problem you need to be aware of possible pitfalls you could encounter. Be aware and proactive. Focus on:

1. Reprioritizing one's life and goals.
2. Focus on the here and now.
3. Take one day at a time.
4. Become more sensitive and thoughtful and loving (especially toward yourself).
5. Realize your personal strengths and competence.
6. Realize the importance of healthy relationships with food, people, the environment, etc.
7. Resolve conflicts without food or self-sabotage. Develop and use new coping skills, some of which I believe you are now aware of and are in the process of internalizing.

In order to grow, one must say goodbye to the negative behavior. Although this feels different and painful, it brings with it a renewed acceptance of YOU in life. Through the grief you experience, you will be able to experience gratitude. To be grateful for having experienced what you have can lead to a new sense of purpose for you. Was it your purpose to spend the time, money, emotions on your eating problem? Only you can answer that but if you are reading this book it appears to me that you want to experience positive change.

This step of Belief/Acceptance opens a door in your life that has been closed or misused in the past. The ability to image and focus on this change is important in its acceptance. Specific suggestions to help you on this journey will be depicted in the section on Tools of the Trade. During this process you will be more aware of the following. It is what I call a progression table:

1. You first acknowledged the discomfort and problems you experienced in your relationship with food. Chances are that is why you began this journey.
2. Next you recognized the problem after you repeated it again. You felt terrible but....

3. Next you recognized what you were doing while you were in the midst of acting on it but you were unable to stop it at that point.

4. Then you recognized when you were about to repeat the negative behavior and fall victim to it. The difference is you stopped it before it stopped you from being free of it.

The Story of Geraldine

Geraldine is a 23-year-old female who originally sought treatment during summer break of college. As her eating problem worsened, she knew that she was on a path of self-destruction. During her high school years, she had participated in gymnastics, which emphasized low body weight causing her to drop 25 pounds. Through medical and nutritional guidance, she gained weight but a cycle of all or nothing eating, and bulimia ensued for over three years. She stopped participating athletically which had been a major part of her identity, thus an empty and depressed feeling followed. During the treatment process, it became evident that Geraldine had not effectively grieved the loss of her earlier identity as a gymnast. With a five-week window before school was to begin, she diligently worked on this issue. She used our sessions, specific writing exercises and journaling to help. She was determined to work on the steps indicated above and did so. Our contact continued via video and telephone. She wanted to adapt to a life without the use of her eating problem. She no longer binges and purges but uses food periodically within acceptable parameters. She no longer feels powerless and the level of acceptance and reality about the part food plays in her life is clear. She accepts and believes in herself and is optimistic and realistic about her future. Geraldine refers to this template to stay grounded and in control which helps her move one foot forward at a time.

I urge you to be aware that you are saying goodbye to that part of yourself that has used these negative behaviors, thoughts, and feelings for years. This is a loss, albeit a healthy and positive one, but still a loss. Recognizing this, acting on it and changing it ultimately has been your goal and desire. The need to grieve it facilitates the process of change thus the acceptance of it.

As you journey through the steps presented, you will understand this belief/acceptance phase. You will no longer need your negative relationship with food to be the main focus of your life. You will want this new relationship to grow. As you continue to strengthen it you will find yourself growing as a loving, tolerant, spiritual, and optimistic human being.

The focus on food and the emotions you shared with it in the past will change. Will you miss it and experience some doubts you had while on this journey? My wish for you is to internalize this newfound freedom. Life is not static thus life with food will not always be static. Perhaps you will need to review the steps again. But remember you will know how good it feels to keep that healthy relationship. Those thoughts and the experience you had with them will help you get over an occasional bump now and then. Appreciate your story because it will be key to moving forward in a new way. Focus on the positive not the negative, and ask yourself those three questions presented throughout this book again, namely:

- Are you ready and willing to understand and change your relationship with food?
- Are you ready to focus on the feelings of loss that will surface?
- Are you willing to grieve that which surfaces as you go forward?

Stay the Course. Love Yourself. Believe in Yourself. Allow Yourself to Be Who You Were Meant to Be. Your success is yours, but it can also touch others who know you. Be authentic, embrace the steps written in this book and find compassion in yourself, I wish you peace within.

Points to Remember

1. Belief has been defined as confidence, truth, trust, and faith in something. One must believe that you can change your relationship with food, and you must believe in yourself.

2. Understand and be aware of what you believe in, that will alter what you believe you deserve.

3. This step Belief/Acceptance opens a door in your life that has been closed or misused in the past. You will experience a sense of gratitude you might not have experienced in the past.

4. The Progression Table above, read it, understand it, act on it.

5. Be aware that you are saying goodbye to that part of yourself that has used these negative behaviors, thoughts, and feelings for years.

6. Life is not static thus life with food will not always be static.

PART 4

SUMMARY

"Begin to be now what you will be hereafter"
-William James

SUMMARY

MY MAJOR PURPOSE for writing this book was to call attention to the effect of loss on disordered eating. It is an area that has been touched upon that I believe needs more awareness and treatment. The text addresses losses in our life that lead to a void, causing the increase in eating problems. This can be in the form of not eating, binging, purging, compulsive eating, and overeating all of which lead to a negative relationship with food.

In addition, this text calls attention that when we try to change our relationship with food, the issue of loss resurfaces, and this must be dealt with. These facts have encouraged me to suggest the Template for Change elaborated in this book. I have outlined six steps, some, or all of which, will be useful in changing your relationship with food if you embrace them. Questions we hear repeatedly are "why can't I sustain the changes made in my relationship with food?" Again, I believe we need to acknowledge and grieve the loss this change represents. This template outlines specific steps to focus on. By creating this template, one has a roadmap by which to encourage change. You have the flexibility to explore these steps and acknowledge the relevance of them. This creates a specific structure that has within its parameters flexibility to explore and make needed personal changes. The above summarizes one's relationship with food, shame, anger, fear

& anxiety, inner voices, belief & acceptance. In each step I have summarized their underlying definitions, its' possible effects, and case examples to help clarify them.

The introduction to this book begins with a letter written by Eda LaShan in her book Winning the Losing Battle: Why I Will Never Be Fat Again (1979). This book has resonated with me for all these years. This book, my work as an Eating Disorder Specialist, as well as my experiences professionally and personally, have been the reason that I have spent so much of my life trying to shed light on Loss and Eating Problems. Although, Ms. LaShan referred to weight gain, I believe her message should be included in regard to each and every eating problem. She addressed such topics about the agony of being fat, obesity and trauma, finding oneself, dieting and dealing with change. She focused on giving her problem a decent burial in order to give up her fat self, "or the neuroses involved therein" (p.162). She believed that this was her most important and dramatic insight about why people gain weight back. She stated that is the case "because we have not taken the time to mourn for someone of great importance-our fat self" (p.162). She recognized she was mourning and saying good-bye to the Eda who suffered and experienced most of her life with an eating problem causing her to be obese for so many years. She allowed herself to feel the sadness of letting go but also the joy of letting this part of her go.

My message to the reader is that no matter what the eating problem is, allow yourself to let it go, while nurturing the Self each and every day to follow. Be true to the real You!

Everything happens for a reason: I do not know what your philosophy is on this but I firmly believe that Saying Goodbye to your original relationship with food leads you to say Hello to a life you may have dreamed of or thought about; now you can pursue it. The strength you have will be realized as you move through this journey of loss, grief, and acceptance.

Let this be the beginning of your journey. Good Luck!

Points to Remember

1. My major purpose for writing this book was to call attention to the effect of loss on disordered eating. It is an area that has been touched upon that I believe needs more awareness and treatment.

2. This Template for Change laid out is my roadmap by which to encourage change in this area.

3. This book represents a renewal from a conflict-ridden relationship with food to a balanced, loving relationship filled with realistic and positive optimism.

4. My wish is that food and eating become normalized and balanced and not as an "all or nothing" experience which leads you to feel it is impossible to attain.

5. Hopefully, my personal story written in the section To My Readers will resonate with you and be helpful on your journey.

APPENDIX A

TOOLS OF THE TRADE

THE FOLLOWING PART focuses on, what I refer to as a toolbox that is filled with various exercises and facts that can help you on this journey. As with any toolbox it is important that it is filled with what you may need when you need it. Some of these tools you may have, perhaps you used them or forgot that they were there. Many may be new to you. I hope you will find them useful as you grieve and say goodbye to the old relationship with food. I urge you to use them when needed and add significant tools personal to you.

Toolbox

1. **Stop, look**, and **listen** - Remember to **Stop** before you leap. **Look** at what is happening both around you and within you. What is in the present and ahead of you? **Listen** to your inner voice, as well as what the outside world is saying.

    This exercise helps you to be mindful of what you are about to do. This will enable you to be aware of the situation and respond accordingly. This allows you to distance yourself from the situation or feeling. This helps to balance impulsive and compulsive behaviors as well as take responsibility for your actions.

2. Eat like a lady or gentleman – Focus on eating with a certain sense of what I refer to as "class". What do I mean? Eat with utensils where needed. When eating finger foods do it without stuffing your face. Taste the Food and allow yourself to enjoy it. Always be MINDFUL.

3. Do not scratch the itch – The following exercise will help you understand this quote. It also serves as a reminder not to eat compulsively or to eat without awareness. It is also tied in with the **stop, look** and **listen** approach.

    Notice when you have an itch perhaps on your arm. Be aware of it but do not scratch it, rather wait and focus on the feeling. Usually the feeling goes from an itch to a needle like pain. Stay with it, you will experience that the pain and the itch is no longer noticeable. This exemplifies what happens if you do not use food or starvation to eliminate a feeling. Feel it, that feeling will pass, you will feel emotionally fulfilled with hope and gratitude.

4. Focus on your senses – Our senses are not used as often or effectively as we can. Focus on them and allow them to enhance your life.

    Sight - Awaken your sight. See what you want, don't want and what is present. Open your eyes do not turn your head. Notice the beauty of places, people, and things. Remember that there is an I behind every EYE. Smell – Smell the scents of freshness and newness. Allow yourself to smell the food you eat this will make eating more satisfying and enhance taste. This is okay, allow it. Taste – Allow yourself to taste and savor the food that you are eating now, enjoy it. Do not overeat or under eat. Be honest about how much you taste. Taste Success. Hearing – Listen to yourself and your Inner Voice. Listen to what others are saying. Hear the wind, birds, music and all that life has to offer. Touch – Allow in feelings and to be touched by joy as you touch others. Enjoy cuddling and hugging with those you love and care for. Allow yourself to hear, feel, taste, smell, touch that which you desire and see.

5. "Music is moonlight in the gloomy night of life" Jean Paul. Music is a personal favorite of mine. It enlightens me and strengths me in so many ways and helps me to stay on my journey of success even when I find myself taking a detour. It utilizes the sense of hearing.

6. Relaxation - Through relaxation one becomes more able to focus and do. It enhances a level of energy and understanding about the situation at hand. It helps the senses to do what they do best. I encourage the use of meditation to relax. Help to manage your stress and energy level. The awareness of what challenges our ability to move forward is another gift from relaxation and meditation. There are various apps and books that endorse and describe meditative exercises. Allow yourself the time to use them.

7. Procrastination – Are you procrastinating? Ask yourself if you are feeling overwhelmed with the task. Do you fear failure or success? Do you feel unsure about the future? Write down any thoughts or feelings about this. Being

aware of them is a step to move forward. Take baby steps, use positive self-talk, and acknowledge the process.

8. Imagery and visualization - I have always believed that in order to effect change we need to be able to visualize it. One needs to see the image of what you want. Staying focused on that image will help to guide you to that end. If you want to be free of the dysfunction of your eating problem; and develop a new healthy relationship with food, you must be able to see it in your future. The visualization can help you to journey through the pain and loss you may be experiencing. Keep your mind's eye on what you truly want for yourself. An exercise I suggest is to visualize saying goodbye to the part of you with the negative behavior and its past meaning. Actually wave goodbye to this image. You may feel the pain of it because that is the loss and grief you may be experiencing. Hopefully, you will see the positive of it. If you hold on to the image of what will follow, you will survive and embrace the new. It is important for you to focus on this and keep steadfast to this end. Say goodbye to the old and hello to the new. This visualization enhances your imagination to create what you want. You know what I mean. Don't you?

The foundation of this book includes the steps to understand yourself, grieve the losses experienced and move toward a healthy existence. The use of creative visualizations helps you to believe in yourself and your future. Allow yourself to be creative and paint a realistic picture for your future. Creative Visualization by Shakti Gawain (2001) suggests four basic steps for effective creative visualization, they are: set your goal, create a clear idea or picture, focus on it often, and give it positive energy.

9. Remember first came the idea of what you want, then came the choice and decision to pursue it but then came the action to carry it out. You must go into Action mode to fulfill the goal.

10. Be aware and mindful not to get in the way of yourself. Keep it simple, stay humble, practice gratitude, ask for help if you need it and take it one day at a time

11. Journaling can be very helpful. It becomes a vehicle to express your thoughts and feelings. This helps you to communicate with yourself.

12. Write up the Newsletter about yourself. It should exemplify your journey, your failures, and your successes.

13. In *A Better Way to Live* (1991) Og Mandino states we can all be divided into three main classes.

    1. Those with Willpower (leaders).
    2. Those with Desire, their intentions are good but do not exercise the necessary action and dominance to win. They wish but not demand (of themselves).
    3. Those people of Fate (they give up and say that things will never come their way).
        Ask yourself where you are in this lineup and where you want to be.

14. Be aware of what your intentions are, within its definition is what you hope for.

15. What is your attitude? Please focus on attitude, believe in it. Attitude is a way we feel or think about things. It could be about people, places or things. Be aware of your attitude in life! The way we see and think of things definitely impacts what and how to structure and live our life. Each day ask yourself what is your attitude? It can make all the difference in the outcome.

BELIEVE IN YOURSELF, WORK THROUGH THE LOSS AND GRIEF NEEDED TO ATTAIN AND MAINTAIN THAT BELIEF.

APPENDIX B

ADDITIONAL BOOKS FOR YOUR PERSONAL BOOKSHELF

BELOW IS A limited list of books that stress wellness and call attention to the contents of my book. They include my summary of each book. These books are literally the tip of the iceberg of good literature about wellness and eating problems. If you chose to read any of them, I hope they will enhance your body of knowledge on this subject. They are:

1. Goodbye ED, Hello Me, Recover from Your Eating Disorder and Fall in Love with Life, by Jenni Schaefer

    This book calls attention to the relationship Jenni had with Ed (eating disorder) and how she moved past it. It is an inspiring and informative book and journey.

2. French Toast for Breakfast: Declaring Peace with Food, by Maryanne Cohen

This book is a guide for those who are concerned with their eating issues. The author creates an informative and interesting book to help begin the healing process.

3. Necessary Losses: The Loves, Illusions, Dependencies and Impossible Expectations That All of Us Have to Give Up in Order to Grow, by Judith Viorst

    This is a classic book that calls attention to what one needs to give up in order to grow in the face of loss.

4. Everything Happens for A Reason: Find the true meaning of the Events in Life, by Mira Kirshenbaum.

    This book stresses solutions for people to achieve a more functional life. Exploration into this subject is intended to find meaning in the events we experience in our life.

5. Mindfulness for Beginners, by Jon Kabat-Zinn.

    Whether you are a beginner or active believer of Mindfulness you will find this book engaging and informative. It allows one to focus on mindfulness and the need to stay present.

6. Keep Calm and Carry On, by Mark A Reinecke

    This is a lovely book showing you ways to Keep Calm. It can serve as a handheld reference to be used when needed.

7. It's Never Too Late..., by Patrick Lindsay

    This inspiring book lays out 172 simple acts to change your life. He summarizes his insights with a famous quote. This book has been in my bookshelf for years.

8. The Four Agreements, by Don Miguel Ruiz

    The author lays out 4 agreements to live by. If you desire to live a life of fulfillment you must find the courage to break past fear-based beliefs to claim your personal power and authentic self. I find this book to be a powerful book that may represent a spiritual message for many.

AFTERWARD - COVID 19

"In a dark time, the eye begins to see."
- Theodore Roethke

IF YOU ARE reading this section, you have heard my message. Although it represents the ending of this book, I sincerely hope that it will represent the beginning of a relationship with food that is positive on all levels, physically, mentally, emotionally, and spiritually.

The steps outlined have been designed to help you on this journey to say goodbye to your dysfunctional relationship with food. They are to be referred to and used when and as needed. Life is so much more than food. Life is to be cherished and understood during both the good times and the bad. Food is not the culprit, the relationship with it is.

I would be remiss if I didn't include the following. I sent this manuscript to my publisher during the month of May 2020. The time was dark and worrisome because we were in the middle of a Pandemic. The virus Covid 19 had collided with life as we knew it. The need to stay isolated and socially distant was the strong and necessary message to all of us. It has been a time of fear, anxiety, and anger. It has been a time when many looked for ways to be positive, and optimistic. However, it also represented a time when eating increased for most.

I was struck by the timing of this book. Could the reality of the situation led to or add to disordered eating? We were inundated with loss in multiple realms. My answer was "yes" it could be and did add to increased disordered eating for many. I needed to get my message out. Although there were so many losses, this Pandemic also represented how life is special and should be appreciated, and healthy. Those who used food to isolate in the past would hopefully understand how destructive this was. The isolation due to the Covid 19 was superimposed isolation for some. For others, this isolation was new and difficult. This time could also be used to be mindful of what to eat, how to eat it and how to enjoy it. How you use your time and what you want is a question you can explore.

Due to this virus I ask you to be aware of what your relationship with food was before the Pandemic, during it and now as things are beginning to loosen up. Although uncertainty still exists, things seem to be more optimistic. Please ask yourself if you want to let this rob you of life. This is a time to understand your relationship with food. As stated above, food is not the culprit. You can and should be comfortable and enjoy what you eat. However, if you have been eating uncontrollably, or restricting foods, and want to change it, use the steps outlined in this book. It can help you journey to a way of eating that is liberating, fulfilling and permanent, more than you have had in the past. Grieve the loss of the old ways and release that negative self. Be proud of yourself and move forward. In addition, be gentle with your grief and tame the inner critic.

My message would have been the same if there was no Pandemic. However, let's look at all the aspects of it and move forward. The message is that Life is too special to lose! Do not let any eating problem rob you of Life!

BIBLIOGRAPHY

Berne, Eric MD. 1978. *Transactional Analysis in Psychotherapy*. New York: Ballantine Books.

Erikson, Erik H. 1980. *Identity and the Life Cycle*. New York: W.W. Norton & Co.

Finley, Guy. 2000. *Freedom from the Ties that Bind, The Secret of Self Liberation*. Minnesota: Llewellyn Publications.

Gawain, Shakti. 2002. *Creative Visualizations Use the Power of Your Imagination to Create What You Want in Your Life*. California: New World Library.

Kirshenbaum, Mira. 2004. *Everything Happens For a Reason*. New York: MJF Books.

LaShan, Eda. 1979. *Winning the Losing Battle, Why I Will Never Be Fat Again*. New York: Thomas Y. Crowell.

Lerner, Harriet. 1997. *The Dance of Anger, A Woman's Guide to Changing the Patterns of Intimate Relationships*. New York: Harper Collins.

Mandino, Og. 1991. *A Better Way To Live*. New York: Bantam Books.

Parente, Louise. 1998. *Fathers, Daughters and Eating Disorders*. UMI Dissertation Services.

Rubin, Theodore Issac. 1970. *Forever Thin*. Seattle: Thrift Books.

Schwartz, Richard. 2017. *Internal Family Systems*. Wisconsin: PESI Publishing Media

Zerbe, Katherine. 2003. *The Body Betrayed: A Deeper Understanding of Women, Eating Disorders, and Treatment*. California: Gurze Books.

Zonnebelt-Smeenger, DeVries, Robert C. 2001. *The Empty Chair, Handling Grief on Holidays and Special Occasions*. Michigan: Baker Books.

CPSIA information can be obtained
at www.ICGtesting.com
Printed in the USA
FSHW012106061020
74494FS

9 781982 254162